Where Have You Gone?

TEXAS LONGHORNS

Whit Canning

www.SportsPublishingLLC.com

ISBN: 1-58261-952-2

All playing-day photographs provided by the University of Texas.

Publishers: Peter L. Bannon and Joseph J. Bannon
Senior managing editor: Susan M. Moyer
Acquisitions editor: Mike Pearson
Developmental editor: Elisa Bock Laird
Art director: K. Jeffrey Higgerson
Dust jacket design: Kenneth J. O'Brien
Interior layout: Kenneth J. O'Brien
Imaging: Kenneth J. O'Brien, Heidi Norsen, and Dustin Hubbart
Photo editor: Erin Linden-Levy
Vice president of sales and marketing: Kevin King
Media and promotions managers: Mike Hagan (regional),
        Randy Fouts (national), Maurey Williamson (print)

Printed in the United States of America

Sports Publishing L.L.C.
804 North Neil Street
Champaign, IL 61820

Phone: 1-877-424-2665
Fax: 217-363-2073
www.SportsPublishingLLC.com

CONTENTS

Preface vii

Acknowledgments ix

Scott Appleton 2

Bill Bradley 9

Mike Campbell 16

Tom Campbell 22

Duke Carlisle 29

Raymond Clayborn 36

Jack Collins 40

Mike Cotten 45

Gib Dawson 51

Chris Gilbert 57

Jerry Gray 63

A.J. "Jam" Jones 68

T Jones 73

Ernie Koy Jr. 78

Bobby Lackey 85

Roosevelt Leaks 92

Alan Lowry 97

Bud McFadin 101

Bob McKay 105

David McWilliams 111

Richard Ochoa 118

Randy Pechsel 123

Ben Proctor 129

Rene Ramirez 136

James Saxton 142

James Street 147

Ben Tompkins 154

Byron Townsend 159

Johnny Treadwell 166

Julius Whittier 171

Bobby Wuensch 177

PREFACE

When I met with Johnny Treadwell for the opening interview for this book, he felt obliged to warn me that he was extremely leery of sportswriters and media types in general. To which I replied, "That makes two of us."

From that point, our relationship proceeded in splendid fashion, as was the case with an additional 30 interviews that followed. In some instances the end result is slightly askew of original plans, but it was a lot of fun.

The assignment was to update the lives of a number of former Texas players who have been generally absent from the public eye in recent years but are well remembered by the Longhorn faithful.

To that end, I turned the calendar back 20 years and traveled backward through time from that point. So the youngest Longhorn in the book—Jerry Gray—played his last season at UT in 1984.

Within that time frame, it is not surprising that the majority of the individuals in the book played their UT football for Darrell Royal and that each played on at least one championship team. But although many were All-Americans or Longhorn legends, this is not presented as a comprehensive look at the greatest players in Texas history. That would require a much larger book.

But it is often a chronicle of amazing performances against long odds—on and off the field—that have carried Texas teams to their greatest victories and former players to their greatest triumphs in life.

Among these, Treadwell's famed "Now we've got 'em where we want 'em" speech in the 1962 Arkansas game is among the most memorable, setting the tone for the Texas teams of the 1960s and displaying the unique spirit that convinced a generation of Longhorns that no matter how it looked, they were never beaten.

That spirit was also strong in the late Scott Appleton, who through new-found faith and immense personal courage took a life turned upside down and set it upright again, ending his days as a source of strength and inspiration to others.

Elsewhere are Duke Carlisle's three inspired performances during the 1963 national championship season; the improbable comeback against Arkansas in the 1969 Great Shootout; David McWilliams's victory over cancer; James Saxton's triumph over a deadly virus; T Jones's finishing in the Hall of Honor at two schools after once abandoning his career for personal reasons; and many others.

Included, of course, is the journey of Julius Whittier, who came to UT "just looking to have some fun" and became the pioneer of a new era, earned three degrees, and launched a successful law career.

An elite group, one and all, and most enjoyable.

ACKNOWLEDGMENTS

I would like to extend heartfelt thanks to the many people who helped with or contributed to this project. These are:

The former Texas football players who graciously took the time to share the thoughts and memories of their lives that make up the content of this book. Specal thanks to Tresh Steffens, for sharing illuminating and often painful memories for the chapter on her brother, Scott Appleton.

Sheila Eveslage in the T Association office, without whose invaluable contribution this project would have never known lift-off.

My editor, Elisa Bock Laird, a reliable source of guidance, support, and patience.

Sources:
Texas Football Media Guide
Horns, Hogs, and Nixon Coming by Terry Frei, Simon & Schuster, 2002
Bleeding Orange by John Maher & Kirk Bohls, St. Martin's Press, 1991

Where Have You Gone?

TEXAS LONGHORNS

Where Have You Gone?

SCOTT APPLETON

In a windswept cemetery in a town that calls itself "The Heart of Texas," a strange group of mourners gathered 13 years ago to say goodbye to Scott Appleton.

Included among those paying final respects were Darrell Royal, his former coach, and David McWilliams, his longtime friend. Also in the crowd was a grown daughter who had never known him.

Possibly there were also several that day who felt that they had known him twice.

By every conventional yardstick, Appleton was a man who had destroyed himself—his life a grim testament to the pressures of fame and the bitter rewards of alcohol abuse.

Once he had been the bell cow of a national championship team at Texas—a consensus All-American, the winner of the Outland Trophy, and a first-round draft pick. A few years later, he seemed destined to drink himself to death.

But unlike most thus fated, he also rose from the depths of despair.

Finally a miracle occurred in a San Antonio church. The common explanation is that he found God.

More correctly, Appleton himself might say that God found him.

"It wasn't pretty," Appleton said in an interview about a year before his death. "I left pro ball, and one year after I had been on top of the world, I was living in a $60 a month apartment in San Antonio. Me and about 100 roaches.

"Finally I wound up flipping burgers in a McDonald's, the lowest man on the totem pole. I had teenagers telling me what to do.

"Then one night, a Baptist preacher walked in carrying a Bible, and he saved me. I was reborn.

"Alcoholism is a horrible thing, and it almost killed me."

Maybe it did. Appleton died in March 1992 of heart disease—specifically, an enlarged heart. Diagnosed only a few months earlier, he was on a transplant list, awaiting a new heart when the one he had gave out.

SCOTT APPLETON
Hgt: 6-3 • Wgt: 240 • Hometown: Brady

Years played: 1961-1963
Position: Offensive tackle, defensive tackle
Highlights: 1962: All-SWC; 1963: All-SWC, Consensus All-American,
Outland Trophy winner, Cotton Bowl Defensive MVP, finished fifth in
Heisman Trophy voting

He had lived barely 50 years. But somehow he had managed to cram three distinct lives into that span.

In the first, he was the quintessential football hero—the pride of the Brady Bulldogs and Texas Longhorns—a jovial giant with a prankish sense of humor and little notion of the concept of defeat.

In the second—anguished over a failed career, a failed marriage, and his father's suicide—Appleton took a free-fall into the bottom of a whiskey bottle.

Miraculously there was a third. Saved by a street preacher, he put down the bottle and never picked it up again. He began a ministry, and when he died, he left behind boxes containing thousands of grateful letters from young people whose lives he had touched.

As a high school senior in Brady, a town that lays claim to being the exact center of Texas, Appleton played on a team that lost to Stamford 19-14 in the 2-A state finals (Stamford later forfeited because of an ineligible player) and was recruited by the usual suspects.

"We lived on a ranch for a while on the San Saba River, running cattle and sheep, but we also had a place in town," says Appleton's sister, Tresh Steffens, now an Austin realtor. "Scott was my older brother, and he was very focused, very dedicated.

"Our life was focused around football from the time he was in junior high. In high school, Brady had winning teams every year, and on Friday nights you couldn't find anything open in town. Everyone had closed up and gone to the football game.

"There's nothing like high school football in Texas. We just always had a lot of fun.

"During recruiting we had people coming in every weekend, including Darrell Royal and Mike Campbell from Texas and Bud Wilkinson from Oklahoma. It got to the point where coaches were calling ahead to see what my mother was having for dinner.

"I was kind of leaning toward OU, because Coach Wilkinson always brought these cute football players with him. Nevertheless, we were all thrilled when Scott signed with Texas."

McWilliams and Appleton met and became friends when they played together in the high school all-star game. They went through UT together and were roommates in their senior year.

"Scott had gotten married in high school," McWilliams says. "But about midterm in our first year at Texas, they divorced. They were both young kids and just looked at it and said we need to get out of this. It was a mutual agreement and wasn't any big deal.

"We would go hunting and fishing a lot. I would go out there with him to Brady, or he would come up to Cleburne with me. He was kind of a joker. He loved to pull stuff on people and laugh, and he was very competitive—whether it was pitching pennies or jumping steps or whatever. It wasn't about winning—he didn't get mad if you beat him. He just liked doing stuff like that, and he loved those Brady Bulldogs—every Saturday, he had to check and see how they did.

"His father was an alcoholic—a real nice man, kind of quiet—but he was on that alcohol pretty good. Alberta, his mother, was the one who ran the family, and she was a real competitor. About the only drinking Scott did then was a beer or two playing poker."

At that point, Steffens recalls, alcohol was not a big part of her brother's life.

"I was a freshman at UT the year he was a senior," she says, "and if I was at a frat party or something and one of the football players was drinking a beer, he would say, 'Tresh, don't you tell Scott about this.' In those days, he was a dedicated athlete."

Appleton and McWilliams were captains (along with Tommy Ford) in 1963 when the Longhorns went unbeaten and won the national championship with a stunning 28-6 victory over Navy in the Cotton Bowl in a matchup of the top two teams.

Appleton was a consensus All-American, won the Outland Trophy, was named Defensive MVP in the Cotton Bowl, and was drafted in the first round by both the Dallas Cowboys (NFL) and Houston Oilers (AFL). He signed with Houston.

He was truly a colossus bestriding his known world. But by the end of the 1960s, that world had changed drastically.

"I didn't see much of him during that time, until I came back to Austin to join Coach Royal's staff in the early 1970s," McWilliams says. "I did know that he got married in New Orleans in about 1965 and had a daughter. But he got on the whiskey so bad, his wife finally just left."

"It was a very bitter divorce," Steffens recalls. "She remarried several times after that and made it almost impossible to see Scott's daughter [Tanya]. It was heart-breaking."

Appleton lived the rest of his life without knowing his child. But on the day he was buried, she stood at his grave.

"She came to the funeral—a tall, beautiful girl," McWilliams says. "She said she never knew her father, because her mother wouldn't let her see him. But she wanted to be at the funeral."

Appleton's pro career lasted five years, three with Houston and two with the Chargers. McWilliams recalls an early visit when Appleton emerged from the Oilers' locker room with a case of beer on each shoulder and an order to gain 30 pounds. Steffens recalls that on the family's first visit to Houston, they received a case of beer from owner Bud Adams. And by the time he finished in San Diego, Appleton was acquainted with steroids.

Steffens and McWilliams agree that Appleton quickly became disillusioned with pro ball, which was a cold-hearted business lacking the fervent spirit he had known in high school and the camaraderie he had enjoyed in college.

"He was also embarrassed that he had not performed up to expectations," McWilliams says. "He told me once that he felt he had let us all down."

One night in 1973, McWilliams says, "I got a call from Tresh. She said her father had committed suicide, shot himself in the head. She said he had been depressed, and they had tried to hide the guns, but he found one and used it.

"I drove from Austin to Brady in about two hours. When I got to the house, Scott was out in the yard with a fifth of Ancient Age, drinking. I tried to remind him that his father had just killed himself on that stuff, but he wouldn't listen, wouldn't stop.

"We stayed up all night, talking. He wouldn't eat; he just drank whiskey. I left the next morning."

Appleton kept drinking.

"My father was a good man," Steffens says, "but a bad alcoholic. At that point, he was depressed—desolate. He had made a lot of money and then lost it in the stock market and various ways, and he just couldn't go on. I understand that. I've been depressed, too. It took me 20 years to get over that.

"It was hard on my mother. She was a strong woman—Alberta Matilda Leifeste Appleton—and she was notorious. She was an R.N. and was always helping someone. She loved people, and she was a liberated woman before it was in vogue.

"She would fly to football games alone to see Scott, because my dad was an alcoholic, back when women from small towns just didn't do that. She never missed a game and never met a stranger.

"But she had two alcoholics in the house, and it was rough. She finally told Scott, 'You need help.'"

For several years after that, McWilliams says, he never saw his friend sober.

"One time I was at a coaching clinic in Graham, and he came over and spent a few days with me," McWilliams says. "Every day at 10 a.m. he'd go buy a fifth of Ancient Age. He drank a little Coke with it. He would not eat or sleep until he finished that whiskey. He was with me for three days and drank three fifths of whiskey.

"He wouldn't listen to anybody. Finally he quit calling, quit talking to us, just disappeared."

Appleton had gone to San Antonio, where his uncle, A.J. Leifeste, himself a reformed alcoholic, let him use a small rent house he owned.

"Scott had no money, no job; he had lost his career, his family, everything," Steffens says. "He lived in that little rent house of my uncle's. He tried AA and all the traditional things that people do—but he was never anonymous. Everybody knew his name, and he was embarrassed. After being on top of the world, he was in an institution for alcohol rehabilitation."

He worked in fast food joints, as a cook at the Dairy Queen, a McDonald's, and a catfish restaurant. When McWilliams visited him, he says, "He refused to let me give him a ride home. He said, 'I don't want you to see where I live.'"

Then Appleton found the Fourth Street Inn and Dr. Jimmy Allen.

"The Fourth Street Inn was a street ministry that was part of the First Baptist Church," Steffens says. "Dr. Jimmy Allen was the pastor. They would feed the homeless, but before you ate, they would read scripture to you. Scott became very comfortable with that. He became very attached to Dr. Allen, and they talked frequently."

The next time McWilliams saw Appleton, there was no bottle.

"I asked him about it," McWilliams says, "and he said he had quit, and I asked him, 'How?' He said, 'I have accepted Jesus Christ into my life.'

"It was amazing. I just couldn't believe it. After all those years, all those fifths of whiskey, he just laid it down one day and walked away. Here was a guy who had already tried AA a couple of times and failed. And all of a sudden, he just cold turkey quit."

But Appleton did more than just quit drinking. He put his life back together.

"I remember he went to a seminary somewhere and got ordained," McWilliams says. "Then he became a minister."

He began, Steffens says, with the Fourth Street Inn.

"He did a lot of work with them," she says, "started doing his own ministry, did a lot of youth-oriented things and Fellowship of Christian Athletes-type stuff. Scott always loved people, but he especially loved young people. He believed they were the hope of the future, and that's what he concentrated on. He felt that was where God wanted him to be.

"He also did a lot of traveling on church projects. He preached in places all over the country. A lot of his friends were coaches here and there, and they would call him to come talk to their team or some local group.

"Once he began, he always spoke very freely and candidly about his having been an alcoholic and recovering from it. It was his witness, his testimony. He believed he could help others by describing what he had been through."

Particularly gratifying to Steffens was the effect on the family.

"It was a wonderful thing for my mother," she says. "She was so proud of Scott that he had turned his life around and dedicated his life to helping others. I think she was more proud of him for that than any of those trophies he won years ago."

And also, that two of the young people he helped most were Steffens's daughters, Stacy and Kacy.

"I had been through a divorce, and after that their father was pretty much absent in their lives," she says. "During the last 10 years of his life, Scott became basically their surrogate father, and he was terrific. He kept up with them, took them places, helped them in so many ways.

"It meant so much to them to have someone in that role that they could talk to and depend on. They even talked to him about teenage things they wouldn't discuss with their mother.

"Losing him was such a blow to them. It was to all of us, but more so to them, particularly Kacy. She was so distraught she stopped going to school for a while."

McWilliams recalls visiting Appleton after he was diagnosed with heart disease.

"At first, he decided not to put his name on the list for a transplant," he says. "When I asked him why, he said he felt good about his life and his relationship with God, and he felt there were people out there who needed a new heart more than he did."

Steffens says that Appleton was eventually persuaded to get on the list and was wearing a monitor when he died.

"He had left a message on my phone that night," she said. "He spoke to two groups earlier in the day and was going to stay home and watch TV that night. That's where he died, sitting in front of the TV. I called him back when I got in but couldn't get an answer. I just thank God that he didn't suffer.

"It's almost every day now that I run into someone who has a child that he touched, and when I went through his things, I found boxes of letters—thousands of them—from young people he had helped.

"Once in his life he had chased dreams of money and success, but he always seemed to want more. But the last 10 years of his life, I don't think I ever saw him that happy and contented, and he didn't drink for the last 12 to 15 years."

After his death, Steffens says, she was talking to a friend who wondered why God had not performed a miracle to save Appleton.

"He did," Steffens said.

In January, Kacy gave birth to her first child—a daughter named Sophia Scott.

Where Have You Gone?

BILL BRADLEY

W hen Bill Bradley received the summons to report to Darrell Royal's office early on a Monday morning, he was not particularly bewildered regarding its import.

"I knew," he says, laughing, "that when you were summoned to Coach Royal's office, three things could happen, and two were bad."

In this assessment, Bradley was precisely on target.

"We had a long talk there in his office," he says. "The gist of it was, he looked me straight in the eye and said, 'Bill, we're gonna make some changes around here—starting with you.'"

Thus ended the storied quarterback career of the man they once called "Super Bill."

But ironically, that meeting in the fall of 1968 was also the catalyst for future success, not that the future was anything Bradley had ever worried much about.

A few years later, as a free safety with the Philadelphia Eagles, he was an All-Pro selection three straight years (1971-1973) and became the first player in NFL history to lead the league in interceptions in back-to-back seasons.

Bradley eventually had a nine-year career in the NFL, including eight seasons with the Eagles. Then he went home to Palestine.

Bought some land. Began living in and operating a country store/service station. No worries.

"Livin' large," he says. "Enjoying life in East Texas."

Then the phone rang, and Bradley soon embarked on a coaching career that has now strung out more than 20 years and taken him to various stops in the NFL, CFL, WFL, and USFL. In addition to a year at UT, he has coached the secondaries of three San Antonio teams—the Gunslingers, Riders, and Texans—plus the Memphis Showboats, Calgary Stampeders, Sacramento Gold Miners, Toronto Argonauts, Buffalo Bills, and New York Jets. He has coached 11 playoff teams (four in the NFL), including two Grey Cup champions at Toronto.

BILL BRADLEY
Hgt: 5-11 • Wgt: 180 • Hometown: Palestine

Years played: 1966-1968
Position: Quarterback, defensive back

He is now "back home" as the defensive coordinator at Baylor, working for old Eagle buddy Guy Morriss.

He and his third wife, Susan—now married eight years—are also buying and building homes for use or for sale, something Bradley has been doing ever since he started playing pro ball.

The basic family home of the moment sits on the Guadalupe River in Spring Branch, near San Antonio, on land Bradley bought before he left the Jets two years ago. Bradley put Susan's two children—Matthew, 18, and Carissa, 15—in school in the area the last year he was in New York, in anticipation of a move.

"I could see it coming," he says. "Now we have a great place to live, two new jobs, and the kids are doing well. Matthew's a quarterback, and he'll walk on at Tarleton State. Carissa is a national honor student and wants to go into acting or modeling.

"Susan has a ladies apparel and urban cowboy shop down in Bulverde, just south of us, called the Sassy Spur. We met on a blind date when I was coaching in Sacramento, and we've been friends and lovers ever since.

"We're building another place up the road to sell, and I've also got a home in Waco and one back in Palestine. I was actually doing this—buying land and properties—from the time I started playing pro ball.

"It's a good sideline to get into, and it gives you income when you're between jobs—and I've been between a few—and it really has enabled me to stay in coaching all these years."

Of the job he has had—here and yonder—for more than two decades, Bradley says, "I love it—it's made me a good living, given me a chance to see the world—go to Europe, live in Canada—to meet people and have fun. It's how I met my wife.

"So now I have a job not too far away from home, working for a guy I've known for 30 years, and I think we've got a shot at turning it around at Baylor. I don't know how far we'll go in the league, but we're getting better, and I think we can get to a point of playing in bowl games."

The journey that got Bradley to this point began in 1964, when he led Palestine to the 3-A state title and was not merely All-State but All-America, and recruited by every major power this side of the Soviet Union.

"I've still got that All-America patch," Bradley says, "and I've still got a lot of letters from people like Woody Hayes, Ara Parseghian, and John McKay. It was fun, but a lot of it was also pretty high pressure."

In the championship game against San Marcos, he threw two touchdown passes, scored once, and intercepted three passes. He then became the MVP of the North-South All-Star Game and finally the star of the Texans win over the Pennsylvania All-Stars in the Big 33 game.

That was also where the "Super Bill" tag was pinned on.

"Bobby Layne was coaching us," he says, "and Doak Walker was up there helping him. They put me in in the second half, and I threw some deep balls to Jerry Levias, and we won big.

"After the game, Doak was talking to some writers about me and he said, 'I'll bet if you rip that jersey off, you'll find a big red "S" under there.'

"So when I got to Texas, Jones Ramsey, the SID, picked it up and after that in every interview or news release I was 'Super Bill' Bradley.

"The problem was it was unwarranted. I came into Texas with that name when I hadn't done anything. I never liked it, and none of my friends ever called me that.

"It was a name I never lived up to."

But in the beginning, there were large expectations.

When Bradley and Chris Gilbert were sophomores in 1966, the Longhorns—who had lost eight games in six years from 1959 to 1964—were coming off an uncharacteristic 6-4 finish in 1965. But with the two talented sophomores and a new I Formation attack, hopes were high that the program would return to normal.

"Fred Akers was the offensive coordinator," Bradley says, "and the offense we were running—they called it the I-Sprint Out system—was built around the tail-back and quarterback.

"It was a good system for Chris—he gained over 1,000 yards each of the two years we used it. It also worked real well when I was healthy, but unfortunately that was not the case. I had a knee injury against Indiana in the third game and wasn't much good after that.

"We finished 6-4 but went to the Bluebonnet Bowl and beat Ole Miss 19-0, and Chris and I both rushed for over 100 yards. They had taped the knee up where I was relatively healthy. So we finished 7-4 and didn't feel that bad about it."

Bradley had knee surgery, and there were high hopes for 1967.

"We were loaded," Bradley says, "and 1967 was supposed to be 'The Year of the Horns' according to all those bumper stickers that came out. But I injured my knee again and we opened against USC, and I'm lugging this dead leg around, and they just keyed on Chris."

Texas opened with close losses to USC and Texas Tech, won six in a row, and then finished with losses to TCU and Texas A&M.

"The A&M game was basically to see which of us would go to the Cotton Bowl," Bradley says. "I did not have a good game.

"Early in the game we were backed up at about our 10, looking at about third and seven, and Coach Royal sent in a running play, wanting to just play safe and punt it out.

"I always had the ability to change the play if I thought a different one would work, so I told Ragan Gennusa to run an eight-yard buttonhook—his man was playing way off him—and we'd get a first down. I told the linemen to be sure and keep their hands down.

"One guy wasn't listening, and he raised up and they batted the ball in the air for an interception, and they wound up getting a score off the turnover.

"When I got to the sideline, Coach Royal was really hot and rightfully so. After that, things got worse. I wound up throwing four interceptions, and they won 10-7.

"I'm sure that game was one of the last straws as far as me being on Coach Royal's good side. They had to be asking themselves, 'Can we win with this guy?'

"So we went 6-4 again. After that, we actually got invited to a bowl game, but Coach Royal was not in favor of it. There was a private team meeting where all the talk was about us not being good enough to play in a bowl and how embarrassing the season was. So we actually turned down a bowl bid.

"During the offseason there was a lot of grumbling from UT people about three 6-4s and a lot of pressure was being put on Coach Royal. That's when he moved Akers to the defense and brought in Emory Bellard as offensive coordinator, and he invented the Wishbone.

"I never liked it much myself, but God, what an offense it was."

Bradley's experience with it was brief. The Longhorns tied Houston in the 1968 season opener and then suffered a loss at Tech—during which Bradley was pulled in favor of James Street. Forever.

The meeting in Royal's office took place the following Monday morning, and by that afternoon Bradley—one of the three Longhorn captains—was working out as a backup wide receiver.

"I did not run that offense worth a damn," he says, "Not near as well as it was fixing to be operated. It really started clicking once James started operating it. It was built for him, not for me.

"But I was a captain and my daddy taught me not to quit, so I went out to practice. There were five other guys who were moved down that day, and there were a lot of writers and TV cameras out at practice.

"I undid my waist strings, and the first time I went down on a deep route, my sweats fell down around my knees. It cracked everyone up and kind of eased the tension.

"We started rolling with James running the offense, and we never lost again. So I just lined up at backup receiver and did the punting and holding. We got so far ahead against Oklahoma State that they put me in as a receiver, and I talked James into throwing me a touchdown pass in the red zone. He felt sorry enough for me that he did it.

"Then Denny Aldridge, our right corner, got sick. They needed someone, and Mike Campbell put me in there against Rice. On one play I sniffed out a pass and rushed in and hit the receiver and knocked him on his butt about three yards behind the line of scrimmage. The quarterback had to eat the ball, and we got a sack and a fumble recovery and eventually a touchdown out of it.

"When I came off the field, Mike grabbed me and said, 'Bradley, I don't know what you're doing out there—but keep doing it!' So I was a starter in the secondary for the rest of the season.

"Actually, I also wound up really being a team leader, because I wound up every Friday giving the speech to the team about how we were going to beat so-and-so the next day and how well we would do. So I kind of rehabilitated myself."

Which is not to say he abandoned the off-the-wall approach that had thus far carried him through life and into a few doghouses.

"When we got to the A&M game, we were rolling and I was pumped," he says, laughing. "So me, Chris, and Corby Robertson were out there for the pregame coin toss, and we won the toss, and the official looked at me and said, 'Captain Bradley, do you want to kick or receive?' And I said, 'We don't give a shit!'

"I could tell from the reaction that that had not been said to the official before."

But all ended well. Texas won 35-14, and in a remarkable atonement for the previous year, Bradley intercepted four passes—still a UT record.

"Then we went out and annihilated a good Tennessee team in the Cotton Bowl and wound up ranked No. 3 in the nation," he says. "I had an interception, caught a pass, and scored a two-point conversion. I couldn't have asked for a greater finish to my career."

A better finish, he figures, than much of what preceded it.

"I did not have a good career at UT as far as football was concerned," he says. "Now, if you want to talk about partying, drinking, women, motorcycles, I had it. And I was not a good student.

"I think the knee injuries had something to do with the fact that I did not live up to expectations. But as far as my overall career at UT is concerned, it wasn't anybody's fault but mine."

Also, with Bradley, the prank tendency was always close to the surface.

On the occasion of his first knee surgery, he substituted warm apple juice for his urine sample, causing a mild panic at the UT medical center—where his aunt was an administrator—over the belief that a severe diabetic had been scheduled for surgery.

"I did it as a prank on my aunt," he says. "But I'm sure Coach Royal was impressed when he heard about it."

For three years, Bradley had been one of the top punters in the nation, and on that basis the Eagles drafted him. In a blowout game late in his rookie season, he talked a coach into letting him play defense.

"The first time I ever touched the ball in the NFL, other than punting, I intercepted a pass thrown by Roger Staubach and ran it back for a touchdown," he says. "That opened some eyes.

"I was hurt the next year—I've had five knee surgeries in all—but in 1971 I became a starter at free safety."

He had 11 interceptions in 1971 and nine in 1972, making him the first player in history to lead the league in two straight seasons.

"I still put that on my resumé," he says, laughing. "It's a better handle than 'Super Bill.'"

Since then there have been a lot of football jobs and a couple of failed marriages—of which he says, "The first one was my fault—I was a terrible husband. The second one, she left me—broke me down like a shotgun."

But Bradley says his life is straightened out now, and one of the best things about it is the friendship with his old coach.

"We're good friends now," he says of Royal. "In fact, I almost feel like his son. He's a great guy, and I've learned a lot from him. There was a time when it was different, but now we have a lot of fun together."

But all along, for Bradley, having fun was really the point.

"Sometimes people ask me about my ambitions," he says. "Hey, I never had any ambition except just putting one foot in front of another without falling down. I guess at one time I wanted to play professional baseball—I played semipro as a kid—but that was about it. In fact, I think the point at which I really began to enjoy coaching was when I got rid of any notion of being a head coach.

"Ever since then, it's been a lot of fun. I've made a good living, been a lot of places, met a lot of people, had a lot of success. I've got a great marriage, and I'm happy.

"And the greatest thing of all is—I've never worked a day in my life."

Where Have You Gone?

MIKE CAMPBELL

It was New Year's Day 1970, and Mike Campbell was standing on the field at the Cotton Bowl during a TV timeout, waiting to play the final minute of his college career.

It had been an exceedingly good career, all in all, for both Campbell and his twin brother, Tom—especially because it was never supposed to happen. The two were not exactly high-profile recruits coming out of high school and were never figured as college material—let alone starting defensive backs for a national championship team.

But here they were. Back in December, the Arkansas Razorbacks had been vanquished in The Great Shootout, and with 1:08 to play in the Cotton Bowl, Texas had just scored to take a 21-17 lead over Notre Dame.

Life seemed pretty good and—hold it, what's this? Egad, it's those louts from South Bend again.

"We were waiting to kick off after the touchdown, and I was standing near the Notre Dame sideline," Campbell says. "But there was a timeout, and suddenly there was this barrage of really filthy language coming at us from the Notre Dame bench—actually from the area where coach [Ara] Parseghian was standing.

"This had been going on all day. Their coaches, even Parseghian, were constantly yelling at the officials trying to get them to throw a flag on us for something, and they had been yelling at us, trying to intimidate us. Their players were doing the same thing.

"So now they were trying to goad one of us into reacting, so a flag would be thrown and they would get better field position for the kickoff return. I looked over, and there was even a priest standing there in the middle of them. In fact, I'm not so sure it wasn't the priest who was cussing us the loudest."

So, as the stalwart son of parents sometimes known as "Iron Mike" and "Bloody Mary," Campbell responded with the social gesture he deemed most appropriate for the occasion.

MIKE CAMPBELL

Hgt: 5-11 • Wgt: 186 • Hometown: Austin

Years played: 1968-1969
Position: Defensive back
Highlights: Starter on the 1969 national championship team

"I shot 'em the bird," he says.

History does not record whether any of the 75,000 witnesses noticed this salute, but Campbell recalls that the Notre Dame sideline went berserk.

"It was hilarious," he says. "They ran out onto the field and started yelling to the official and waving their arms and pointing at me.

"It was just what they were trying to get me to do, but I made sure nobody saw it. I looked around and made sure where each official was and which way he was facing—then I shielded myself behind one of our guys and did it. They saw it, but the refs didn't. By the time the official looked at me, I had my back to him, looking up into the stands."

Having seen nothing, the magistrate dismissed the charges, and Texas kicked off. Moments later brother Tom's interception ended Notre Dame's last hope, and the championship season was complete.

"They had tried to intimidate us all day, but it didn't work," Campbell says, "and we were just kind of disgusted with it. It was a thrill and an honor to play in that game, but I'll guarantee you, there were no handshakes at the end."

With the Irish vanquished and graduation behind him a few months later, Campbell decided he needed a change of scenery. So he found himself working on an oil rig platform.

In the middle of a jungle in Indonesia.

"I went to work in the oil business as soon as I got out of college, and I've been in it ever since," says Campbell, who now lives in Houston and works for Baker Hughes Drilling Fluids. "The company I was working for at that time had some international positions open—entry level, working on oil rigs—so I jumped at the chance to go off and see the world.

"Austin is an unbelievable place to grow up, but you can get so doggone comfortable at that age, and I wanted so see what else was out there. Austin is probably the greatest place in America to live, but the comfort level had just become too great. It was time to—well, just get out.

"So I spent the next three years working in the jungles of Borneo and Sumatra.

"Actually, I was based in two different cities during that time—Singapore, which is very Westernized and a really pleasant place to live, and Jakarta, which is in Indonesia and is quite different. For a while, I was also in a small town in Sumatra, which was really Third World.

"When I took the job, I didn't even know where those places were. I had to look them up on a map."

But as Campbell soon discovered, there was plenty to do.

"They would fly you by helicopter out to a rig in the middle of the jungle," he says, "and you would stay there for two weeks—with no way out. Sometimes just getting there was an adventure.

"A lot of those helicopter pilots had flown in Vietnam, and they were daredevils. They really liked to give you a ride—they would fly down below the jungle or the riverbeds, and it was really a trip. It could also be a little rough working out on the rigs with the humidity and the monsoons, but if I'd wanted to stay in a cocoon, I would have stayed in Austin. Actually, I liked it."

A big part of that was due to what was available in between trips to the rigs.

"They would put you out there for two weeks, then bring you back and give you two weeks off," he says. "During those two weeks, I could do anything I wanted and go anywhere in the world I wanted.

"I spent a lot of time in Bali, which is everything they say it is—a tropical island paradise. I got off the plane looking for Nancy Kwan and never found her, but other than that it was great.

"I wanted to see a little of the world, and the oil industry provided me the opportunity to do that. On my time off, I went skiing in France and Switzerland, went down to Africa to see the game preserves, just anything I wanted.

"It was a great deal for a guy who was single and 24 or 25 years old. It was everything I wanted going into it."

When he came back, the company sent him to a place he regarded as being stranger than Indonesia.

"They sent me to Oklahoma City," he says, laughing, "and I figured out real quick that if I was going to live there, I'd have to take my T ring off. And that wasn't going to happen.

"So I went back and told my manager, 'There are some things I can't do, and living in Oklahoma City is one of them.' Those are good folks up there, but it's a big rivalry, and I just didn't feel comfortable.

"So I spent three years in Corpus Christi and came back here to The Woodlands, and I've been here ever since."

For the Campbells—whose father, Mike Campbell, was Darrell Royal's longtime friend and defensive coordinator—finishing at UT as starters on a national championship team was, and is, a special memory.

"How did our dad feel about our decision to walk on at UT?" Campbell says. "I don't know if 'horrified' is the right word. That may not be fair. I would say, at the very minimum, 'astounded.'

"We certainly weren't being recruited by anyone. But one thing a lot of people are unaware of is that we were only 17 when we graduated from high school, so all along, the people we competed against were a year older than we were, at least. And at that age, that's huge. Also, at UT we lost what was intended to be a red-shirt year when an assistant coach inadvertently put us into a game.

"Still by the time we were seniors, I weighed 185, and Tom was a couple of pounds lighter. He was a defensive back, and I was playing rover—sort of a combination DB and outside linebacker—and we were plenty big enough for those positions, plus we were as fast as any other defensive back.

"By that time, we had gotten a lot of training from our dad and a lot of strength conditioning from [trainer] Frank Medina. We both played well, and Tom made All-Conference.

"As freshmen, we were at a severe disadvantage, because everyone else was older, bigger, and stronger. But the deal then was that Coach Royal would give a uniform to anybody that asked for one. He would say, 'It's yours until you bring it back to me.'

"That orange and white probably meant a lot more to me and my brother than it did to some other guys, and you don't give something up that means that much. Daddy certainly never showed us any favoritism, but he coached us the same way he did everyone else—relentlessly.

"If you're willing to pay a price and learn—and if you won't quit, you stand a good chance of reaching your goal. For four years, we never took a slow step in practice. And when we took those uniforms, our mom made it clear that we would not be quitting."

For the twins, being the sons of "Iron Mike" Campbell sometimes brought unwelcome comments, which were handled in the usual way.

"I think Tom and I developed a reputation for having some pretty quick fists," Campbell says. "It wasn't really a question of who you could whip, it was a question of what you were willing to take, and we settled that pretty early.

"Growing up, we absorbed a lot from our dad, but I think we also had a natural intensity that came from our mom. She was pretty high strung, and you didn't really fool around with her much. They probably should have called her 'Iron Mary.'"

Both Campbells moved up to the second string—the traveling squad—in their sophomore years but had become starters as seniors. By that time, they were playing on a powerhouse team headed for a momentous showdown.

"After the A&M game, my dad suddenly appeared in front of my locker and stuck out his hand," Campbell says. "He just wanted to shake my hand and say, 'Nice going.' It was the biggest compliment I got from him in four years, and he probably shook everyone else's hand, too, but it meant a lot to me."

On a grim day in Fayetteville 10 days later, Texas ran into a variety of problems. But the unluckiest Longhorn on the field was Campbell—whose assignment for the day involved single coverage against super-swift Chuck Dicus, Arkansas' All-America wide receiver.

"It wasn't anything I wanted, and it certainly wasn't anything my dad wanted, but there was no way around it," he says. "He was by far the greatest receiver I ever covered—on a par with Cotton Speyrer.

"In fact, whenever Cotton and I get together and start kidding around, he always blames me for the fact that Dicus made All-American and he didn't.

"I didn't do a very good job of covering him—he caught nine passes that day—but I did my best."

The consolation is that no one else ever had a good day against Dicus. And in this instance, there was a small moment of retribution at the end.

"I can remember that at the end of the third quarter, I was sitting on the bench and said to whomever was next to me, 'If we don't score pretty soon, we're not going to have time to win this game,'" Campbell says. "On the next play, James Street ran for a touchdown and we were back in it.

"Then they came back on that drive down inside our 10-yard line and could have kicked a field goal, but instead Bill Montgomery threw the pass that Danny Lester intercepted in the end zone.

"The amazing thing about that is that Montgomery was just brilliant all day long—he was rolling out, keeping us off balance, and always seemed to know where to throw the ball. But on that play, he threw a stupid pass, and it cost them big."

Like most members of the defensive unit resting on the bench, Campbell did not actually see the famous Street-to-Randy Peschel pass on the following drive that led to the winning touchdown.

But he does remember that when Royal called the play on the sideline, "My daddy turned and said, 'Aw, hell—defense get ready!'

"He had flown a B-24 in World War II, and nothing much fazed him," Campbell says. "I guess he figured he'd never see anything as tense as what he'd already been through.

"But anytime he saw something he didn't like, that was his reaction: 'Aw, hell.' And he didn't like that call. It seemed a play with no chance to succeed—but it did."

Trailing by a point, Arkansas drove back to the Texas 39, where Montgomery rolled right and looked for his receivers, John Rees and Dicus, who had run identical out patterns to the sideline about 10 yards apart—covered by the Campbells.

After four years of hard work, it is the one play Campbell will never forget. And it was the one time all day that he was praying Montgomery would throw to Dicus.

"That time, I had him covered," he says. "He was boxed in on the sideline and couldn't get away from me.

"It's funny. If you look at the film, it almost looks like a dance. You can see the Arkansas receivers go down the field and make their cuts at the same time. And Tom and I are right with them, making the same cuts, step for step. It looks almost like synchronized swimming or a ballet."

With Dicus covered, Montgomery threw deep for Rees. Brother Tom intercepted, and the game was basically over.

"It was the highlight of my career," Campbell says. "It happened over near our sideline, and Tom and I embraced just for a moment. We had come in four years earlier as scrawny-looking walk-ons and now—for that one brief moment—we were in the spotlight in one of the greatest games ever played.

"Daddy never said anything, but I know he saw it. And I know my mom did. I'm just so happy that we made her proud—that we didn't let her down.

"As for my dad, for all of those 20 years he coached at Texas, with all of the great players he handled—Johnny Treadwell, Tommy Nobis, Glen Halsell and so many others—the greatest coaching job of his life was the one he did on us."

Mike Campbell and his wife, Becky, have been married 25 years and live in The Woodlands. Their daughter, Courtney, just completed her degree at UT, where for three years she was one of the Texas Angels. Mike, 18, is playing football at Sam Houston State, and Collin, 15, is in high school.

Where Have You Gone?

TOM CAMPBELL

Several years ago, Darrell Royal was being probed yet again about the events concluding the 1969 season: the stirring triumph over Arkansas in The Great Shootout that gave Texas the national title and the dramatic Cotton Bowl victory over Notre Dame, which ended a 45-year bowl ban for the Fighting Irish.

The conversation proceeded in orderly fashion through the usual highlights: the 44-yard fourth-down pass from James Street to Randy Peschel that set up the winning score in the Arkansas game (15-14), the 80-yard fourth-quarter march that beat Notre Dame (21-17), the chronicle of clutch offensive plays made with Orange backs against the wall.

Finally, Royal smiled and said, "Well, just don't forget—in both of those games, Tom Campbell saved us."

Yes, indeed, he did.

The final spectacular catch in each game was an interception by Campbell, choking off the last-gasp efforts of both the Razorbacks and Fighting Irish.

The first of the two was particularly riveting—closing out a memorable showdown between unbeaten teams, witnessed by the President of the United States, on a day when the marquee of a Fayetteville church read: "God is a Razorback."

A desperate battle that two states—one elated, the other heartbroken—have never forgotten. Total strangers, upon hearing Campbell's name, still walk up and start talking about it.

"It's been kind of like having your 15 minutes of fame," he says, "except that it's lasted over 35 years."

But when he walked off the field that day, Campbell—now an account executive with Xerox in Austin—never figured he would return to Fayetteville someday and be recognized.

When he did return several years ago, he half expected to find the church marquee proclaiming, "Tom Campbell is a sorry rat."

TOM CAMPBELL
Hgt: 5-11 • Wgt: 183 • Hometown: Austin

Years played: 1968-1969
Position: Defensive back
Highlights: Starter on the 1969 national championship team;
Defensive MVP in 1969 Cotton Bowl

Instead he was welcomed graciously by the coach who suffered the most devastating defeat of his career that day, Frank Broyles.

"When my daughter, Beth, got out of high school, she got a soccer scholarship to, of all places, Arkansas," Campbell says. "So my wife, Kim, and I took her up there to register, but she had gotten there late and was having some problems getting enrolled.

"I was wandering around the athletic complex and happened to walk upstairs to Coach Broyles's office, and he invited me in. We had a very friendly chat—not about the 1969 game—and when I mentioned that Beth was having difficulty getting registered, he swung his chair around and picked up the phone.

"He called the women's athletic director, but she wasn't in. Neither was the assistant AD. He called the soccer coach and he wasn't in, either, but his assistant was. So here's this poor 24-year-old assistant picking up her phone and a voice says, 'This is Frank Broyles.'

"He explained Beth's situation and said he would appreciate it if she would do everything necessary to get his friend's daughter enrolled immediately. And she did.

"The next day the soccer coach was greeting the players and meeting the parents, and I told him I wanted to apologize for causing all the trouble. He laughed and said, 'Yesterday was the most exciting day they've ever had in women's athletics. Coach Broyles has never called here before. The young woman who spoke with him said it was like talking to God.'"

The first time Campbell returned to watch Beth play soccer, a gruff voice behind him suddenly announced, "That's my national championship ring you're wearing."

Campbell turned around and made the acquaintance of Pat Morrison, who had played tight end for Arkansas in the 1969 game.

"He turned out to be a really nice guy, and we became very friendly," Campbell says. "Then last year we had that reunion up there, and all those guys just treated us great. They wouldn't take our money, wouldn't let us pay for anything. They were very gracious hosts, and it was just amazing. Everybody there just had a great time."

Hmmm. Maybe God *is* a Razorback. Who else could muster such Christian charity for a crew that had once caused so much anguish?

And especially the left defensive halfback. Campbell could have sent 20 daughters to the Arkansas soccer team, and it would scarcely have made up for what he did to the Razorbacks in 1969.

On two crucial plays—using nimble feet and hands on one and a nimble brain on the other—he took six Arkansas points off the scoreboard and then killed the Hogs' last hope of kicking a winning field goal.

But before all that could happen, it would require four long years of rigorous training before the twin Campbells—Mike and Tom, sons of Texas defensive coordinator "Iron Mike" Campbell—could be molded into key players on one of the greatest teams in history.

"When Mike and I graduated from [Austin Reagan] High School," Campbell says, "there simply was never any conversation around the house about our playing football in college. Not only did Daddy know we weren't good enough, we knew we weren't good enough.

"We didn't receive a single [recruiting] letter or phone call from any college at any level and didn't expect it. We were two very average high school players who got to walk on at Texas because of our dad.

"I remember him coming into our room one night and saying, 'Darrell has two extra scholarships, and you two can come out and stay as long as you want.' Mike doesn't remember that, and I don't know whether we had scholarships or not, but we stayed.

"But that didn't mean we were going to play—we just weren't ready to quit.

"As freshmen we were listed as defensive ends/split ends, I guess just because everyone had to be on the depth chart somewhere. We weren't big enough to be defensive ends, and if we ever got into a freshman game as split ends, they sure never threw the ball at us.

"As sophomores they made us outside linebackers, and the position finally evolved into rover, which meant we were mainly defensive backs.

"Basically, what happened was that over the years we kept getting better, and the people around us got worse or got hurt.

"Four games into our sophomore year, Mike moved up to the second team, and I made it the next week. I became a starter as a junior, because the guy in front of me got hurt, while Mike was still backing up Corby Robertson. And as seniors, we both started.

"By that time we were 30 pounds heavier than we had been as 17-year-old freshmen, a lot stronger, a lost faster, and a lot smarter. And we felt comfortable about our roles."

In fact, Campbell finished his junior year with two interceptions and the Defensive MVP award in the Longhorns' 36-13 rout of Tennessee in the Cotton Bowl.

And despite what initially seemed long odds, the twins had also had a pair of aces in the hole.

"For us, playing for our dad was pretty much the same as it was for everyone else," Campbell says. "The difference was we had also grown up that way and maybe we were a little bit better prepared to handle it.

"He may have been a little harder on us, I don't know. But we were used to it. He worked everybody hard, and every time you made a mistake, he let you know about it.

"He was tough, and he expected you to do what was required in any situation. Whenever you did something good, he didn't feel that he needed to come around and tell you about it. He assumed you already knew.

"I think he and Darrell were very similar, and that's probably why they got along so well. They trained you to be prepared and do your best, and they threw compliments around like they were manhole covers.

"It's the way Mike and I grew up, which is not to say he was a mean, domineering father. He trained us to do what we needed to do to be the best. We did not take it personally. And no, we did not feel neglected."

Mary Campbell, her son recalls, was pretty much the same way.

"Mentally, she may have been even tougher than he was," Campbell says. "She weighed 100 pounds, and her nickname was 'Bloody Mary.' She prepared us pretty well to play for him. She was in our corner all the way, but she did not baby us."

Neither did ol' dad. But sometimes, little nuggets arrive for those who are in the right place at the right time.

"All the time I played for Daddy, he never once came around and said, 'Nice interception,' or anything like that," Campbell says. "But once I was over at my folks' house visiting, and my dad was on the phone, catching hell from some parent because I was starting instead of her son. Finally, he said, 'Lady, he may not be any good, but he's the best damn thing I've got out there.'

"Having grown up as the son of Mike Campbell, I took that as a compliment, the best I had ever received. I left my parents' house that day feeling really good about myself."

As a desperate battle finally drew to a close in Fayetteville in 1969, many other Longhorns had reason to feel good about Campbell.

But while Campbell's dramatic fourth-quarter interception that sealed Arkansas' fate has been justly celebrated, his role in an equally important play earlier in the game was not fully appreciated for 20 years.

It occurred in the first half when Arkansas—already leading 7-0—apparently scored again on a 26-yard pass from Bill Montgomery to Chuck Dicus, who had beaten double coverage from Danny Lester and Freddie Steinmark.

But across the field, a flag was thrown. John Rees, the other wide receiver, was called for offensive pass interference on Campbell, and the touchdown was nullified.

"What happened looked kind of like a chicken fight," Campbell says. "He was just using his hands to try to block on me like you would do on a running play, which I thought it was, and I was fending him off. The problem was it was a pass, and he was still doing it when the ball was in the air, which was illegal.

"It had no effect on me and certainly had nothing to do with the touchdown play across the field. But then I noticed that one of the officials was looking at us, and I knew that he had seen the play. Otherwise, why would he be looking at me and Rees?

"So I walked over to him and said, 'He's blocking on me after the ball is in the air, and that's pass interference.' And he said, 'You're right,' and threw the flag.

"He really didn't want to throw it, and I don't blame him. But he did."

On the next play the Razorbacks suffered a huge sack and eventually wound up punting the ball away, and the score stayed at 7-0. But although the Longhorns were grateful for the reprieve, it was years later before anyone realized that Campbell had virtually manufactured the call.

"I never mentioned it to anyone," he says, "I certainly never sat down and had a discussion with my dad about the game, I never even watched the film for years and years.

"Finally, about 20 years later I was in a group of people talking, may have been a cocktail party, I don't remember, and I just decided to tell that story. Coach Royal was there, and he overheard me talking about it.

"Still, it was about five years after that that Coach Royal came up to me and started talking about it. He said, 'I'll be honest—when I heard you telling the story that day, I didn't think you were telling the truth, so I went back and looked at the film.'

"On the film, with the wide-angle shot, you could see the whole thing, including me walking up to the official and him dropping the flag. So that's how it finally came out.

"Really, I figured that play evened the breaks, because when Rees caught a 20-yard pass to set up their first touchdown, he was out of bounds when he caught the ball, but the officials didn't call it. So I figured we were even."

But late in the game with Arkansas driving for a possible winning field goal, Campbell took it far beyond even. On a play in which he and brother Mike were framed in identical coverage of the Razorbacks' two wide receivers, the ball came his way.

He stepped in front of Rees with 1:13 remaining and picked it off at the Texas 22-yard line, and The Great Shootout was over.

"It's strange," Campbell says. "Montgomery had been brilliant all day, until that bonehead pass he threw on the previous series that Danny Lester intercepted in the end zone.

"The one I intercepted was a well-thrown pass, but I had good coverage, and in that circumstance he would have been better off just throwing it into the stands. But I'm glad he didn't."

Describing his emotions at that moment, Campbell says, "I think 'elation' would be a good word."

One further adventure awaited: the meeting with Notre Dame in the Cotton Bowl, which Texas won 21-17 by driving 76 yards to score with 1:08 remaining. The brief chance left to the Fighting Irish was snuffed out by—yes, a Campbell interception—with the pass this time being thrown by Joe Theisman. There was a twist.

"This time, I didn't go down," he says. "I was looking for a gold helmet, and the first one I saw, I ran right at him. I hit him a real good lick under the chin and knocked him over backward."

A parting shot in a social atmosphere that was not conducive to fond reunions in the future.

"Notre Dame was a legendary program, and they were a good team," Campbell says. "But we were pretty disappointed with the rest of their act. Their thing was to try and intimidate you, physically and verbally. They would try to push you around, but the worst thing was the abuse coming from their coaching staff on the sideline, including [Ara] Parseghian. They would call you out by name and curse you.

"But Coach Royal had warned us about it, and we just gave it back to them in kind. So I was satisfied to end the game that way."

After UT, Campbell signed a free agent contract with Oakland but didn't stick.

"I had the privilege of being personally cut by John Madden," he says. "He told me, 'Campbell, I think you can play in the NFL—just not with the Oakland Raiders.' After that I was picked up by Philadelphia, but when I was cut at the end of the preseason, I went home, went back, and finished school, majoring in finance.

"I spent a year at a local bank, and I've been in sales ever since, either for someone else or myself, and I've spent a lot of that time in the Brownsville/Corpus Christi area. From 1983 to 1993 I owned my own company, and I've been with Xerox since then."

He and Kim met at UT and were married in 1972 and have two daughters: Kate, 27, and Bethany, 26.

Where Have You Gone?

DUKE CARLISLE

When Texas quarterback Duke Carlisle brought his team up to the line of scrimmage in the second quarter in the Cotton Bowl on Columbus Day 1963, the world looked just about right.

It was the occasion of the annual Texas–OU shootout in Dallas, and as usual, it had drawn quite a crowd. Texas came into the game undefeated and ranked as the No. 2 team in the nation.

Oklahoma was also undefeated and ranked No. 1.

But although it was a showdown between two unbeaten teams at the top of the national rankings, general expectations were somewhat curious. Not many actually gave the Longhorns much of a chance.

Led by whirlwind halfback Joe Don Looney, the Sooners had already beaten defending national champion USC and were fast becoming the darlings of the national scene.

"We had all watched the USC game on TV," Carlisle said, "and although the Trojans put up a battle [17-12], it really wasn't one of those games where you had any doubt who was going to win. OU really looked awesome."

But here were the Longhorns, outplaying the Sooners and sitting on a 14-0 lead midway through the second quarter, having just taken possession deep in their own territory after an OU punt.

At the time, Carlisle's train of thought ran along the lines of "We're doing a great job, let's just keep it going and not do anything to wake these guys up."

And so when the Longhorns reached the line of scrimmage, UT lineman Staley Faulkner got into his stance, looked across the line at massive All-American Ralph Neely, and inquired pleasantly, "Who's No. 1 now, you son-of-a-bitch?"

"I nearly fainted," Carlisle says, laughing. "I thought, 'God, that's just what we need.' The worst thing was we had called an option play to Neely's side, which meant I had to basically run right at him, fake to a halfback hitting the hole, and then slide down the line on the option.

DUKE CARLISLE

Hgt: 6-1 • Wgt: 176 • Hometown: Athens

Years played: 1961-1963
Positions: Quarterback, defensive back
Highlights: Starting quarterback and safety on the 1963 national
championship team; Offensive MVP in the 1963 Cotton Bowl

"So I'm figuring, first he's going to tear the halfback's head off, then he'll tear my head off."

But at the end of the day, all Longhorn heads were still firmly in place, and Oklahoma—beaten 28-7—was no longer the No. 1 team in the land. And if you cared to peruse the postgame accounts, you would learn that on that day, the Russian army couldn't have stopped Duke Carlisle running the Texas option.

The triumph was highlighted by a cover story in *Sports Illustrated* with a photo of Carlisle running the option under a caption that read, "Texas is No. 1."

For Carlisle, a lanky senior from Athens, Texas, who has since built a successful career in the oil business in Mississippi, it was the first performance in an amazing trifecta that capped the perfect season—a national championship.

"A lot was made of our success with the option against OU," Carlisle says, "and a lot of people thought it was a secret weapon we used for that game. Actually we had been running it all year [three games], and I'm sure OU had seen a couple of films of it.

"They had just never faced it. We used Phil Harris, the wingback, as the option back, and he had great speed and was a good runner, and it just worked very well.

"When I came to Texas as a freshman, they were still running the Split-T with the option. But when Darrell Royal switched to the Wing-T in 1961, the option was discarded. That team did so well offensively that it wasn't missed.

"In 1962 our offense looked the same as 1961, but it didn't work the same. We had problems scoring points most of the year. So in 1963 he put the option back in, only we were running it out of the Wing-T."

A month later, Texas was still No. 1 but faced a battle with Baylor that would likely decide the Southwest Conference championship and Cotton Bowl berth, because both teams were undefeated in conference play.

The Bears were led by Don Trull and Lawrence Elkins—who finished the season as the nation's leading passer and receiver, respectively, and were on their way to shattering every existing SWC passing mark.

While these two were leading the high-scoring Bears to lopsided victories, Texas had been carving its way through a schedule of keyed-up opponents with a succession of close wins.

"Each week," Carlisle says, "the sportswriters would come around and ask Darrell what was wrong with the team, and he would get kind of irritated and say, 'Well, we're unbeaten, what more do you want?'

"As for Baylor, their offense was so good you really couldn't stop it—not completely, anyway. But our offense was based on ball control, and that became our plan for stopping the Bears: Run the ball, control the clock, and keep their offense off the field. And it worked.

"Later, I remember [defensive coordinator] Mike Campbell saying one of the prettiest sights he ever saw was looking across the field and seeing Trull on the sideline, loosening up to keep his arm warm because he had been out of the game for so long."

But with Texas leading 7-0 late in the game, the Bears launched a last-gasp drive from their 12 that rolled downfield like a lightning bolt. Carlisle, often praised more as a defensive back than quarterback, had stayed in the game at safety.

"On every play," he says, "Coach Campbell threw an eight-man rush at Trull so he wouldn't have much time to look for receivers. That was fine, except that there were only three of us left back there in the secondary, and it felt a little lonely.

"Finally, they were on our 19-yard line with 19 seconds left and called a timeout. When they came back, everybody knew the next play would decide the game. Our corners were covering the wide receivers, and I was playing the ball.

"When Trull dropped back, I saw him look at Elkins, who broke for the end zone, so I took off after him. I knew with that rush that Trull would have no time to go to a different receiver."

And so, Carlisle, Elkins, and the football all arrived at the back of the end zone together. A photograph of Carlisle making the dramatic game-clinching interception in front of Elkins's outstretched arms became one of the most famous freeze frames in SWC history.

"Actually, the photo I've seen most often has me with my back to Trull and looks like I got there at the last second and barely caught the ball on my fingertips," Carlisle says. "There's another from a different angle that shows me kind of cradling the ball, which is more the way I remember it. I knew I had to get between Elkins and the ball, and I had time to do it."

Joe Dixon, the cornerback Elkins had beaten, came up and thanked Carlisle for saving his butt.

There followed a victory over TCU and another squeaker, 15-13, over the Aggies, with Carlisle scoring the winning touchdown on a sneak in the final minute. Among those observing that game was an Eastern sportswriter named Myron Cope, who would subsequently play a role in one of the biggest wins in UT history.

As a Cotton Bowl opponent, the Longhorns drew the Midshipmen from Navy, a team led by Heisman Trophy winner Roger Staubach and even more exalted than the Sooners had been back in October. For the second time in one season, Texas was involved in a No. 1 versus No. 2 showdown. The difference was that this time Texas was the top-ranked team.

Not that matters changed much. Once again, in the media buildup to the game, the Longhorns came out looking like also-rans. This was mainly due to the pregame hype bestowed on Navy by the Eastern press, led by Cope.

"He'd seen the A&M game, and we had looked bad," Carlisle says. "He was not impressed and began writing columns that basically said we were a counterfeit national champion and didn't have a prayer of staying on the field with Navy.

"He was actually a pretty clever writer, and his columns were easy to read. And every one of them was posted on the bulletin board in our locker room."

A few other things were also going on. In defensive preparations, the Texas coaching staff had instituted the "Staubach Drill," in which a scout team quarterback emulated Staubach's rollouts, the plays on which he was most dangerous. By

Emily and Duke Carlisle (*Photo courtesy of the Carlisle family*)

rolling left or right, he freed himself of the pass rush and gave himself a better opportunity to throw or run—and he did both very well.

Also, in watching the game films, the staff made an astounding discovery:

"When they were on defense," Carlisle says, "on every play you could see a coach on their sideline holding up a big white card—sending in the signals to the defense. It was so obvious that at first you figured it had to be a trick. But it wasn't—you could actually read the cards and know what their defensive scheme would be for each play.

"I remember that when it came out after the game, their coach said he couldn't believe we stole their signals. Actually, he didn't leave us much choice."

Royal once described it as akin to watching a guy standing there waving flags on the deck of an aircraft carrier.

Royal noticed something else on the film—that Navy just sat there in a 5-2 instead of overshifting to the strong side against the Wing-T, which most teams did. The Texas coaching staff knew then that speedster Phil Harris would be alone against the cornerback who, if he focused on Carlisle, would be beaten on the route by Harris, or if he turned to cover Harris, would have his back to Carlisle and lose sight of the ball.

Which led to a game plan that brings a laugh from Carlisle to this day.

"One of the things Cope had written was that the Texas offense was so simple, you could tell when we were going to throw the ball because we switched quarterbacks," he says. "This was because they would usually pull me and put Tommy Wade in if we needed to throw the ball.

"As far as what happened to Navy that day, I guess it was adding insult to injury that it came from the guy who wasn't supposed to throw."

(Carlisle, however, led the team in both passing and total offense).

The final motivational moment came during TV interviews just prior to the kickoff when, as Texas captain David McWilliams recalled, Navy coach Wayne Hardin "made a speech about when the challenger meets the champion, if the challenger beats the champion, then the challenger becomes the champion, or something like that.

"Then they turned the mike on Coach Royal and he just said, 'We're ready.' I was standing next to him, and the hairs on the back of my neck stood up."

By halftime, Carlisle and Harris had worked the pass route for touchdowns of 58 and 63 yards, and Texas was up by 21. The defense boxed Staubach in to the point of –47 yards in sacks by the end of the game, most of them by Outland Trophy winner Scott Appleton.

The final score was 28-6, and Carlisle, in his final game as a Longhorn, threw for 213 yards. It briefly stood as a Cotton Bowl record until Staubach broke it (228) late in the fourth quarter in a lost cause. Appleton and Carlisle, who also scored a touchdown, were the Outstanding Players of the Game.

With his Texas career finished, Carlisle—in the first of many successful financial ventures—briefly became a member of the Green Bay Packers.

"That was during the time when there were two leagues, and things were pretty chaotic," Carlisle says. "Green Bay needed defensive backs, so they drafted me. I was kind of stalling around, so they came up with a signing bonus and a no-cut contract.

"So at a time when college graduates were going to work for $500 a month, I got a $10,000 bonus and a guaranteed salary of $15,000 a year. Of course, in those days they didn't have scouting combines and all the stuff they have now, and they took me basically on word of mouth.

"When I showed up and they saw how scrawny I was, I think it was a shock. But it didn't take Vince Lombardi long to find a way out of the contract. His chance came when the Dallas Cowboys wound up with all of their quarterbacks injured.

"John Roach, the former SMU star, was a year out of pro ball and in the real estate business in Dallas. Green Bay still had the rights to him, so Tom Landry called Lombardi and said he needed Roach badly. Vince said, 'You can have Roach if you take Carlisle, too.' So I drew the $15,000 for one year and then went back to Texas to get my MBA.

"When I was back at Texas, the war in Vietnam was heating up, and I still had military service to do. But I met a guy in grad school who was in the Medical Service Corps, and he told me that you could get a commission if you had an MBA.

"So when I went into the service, I wound up working in hospital administration in Lansduhl, Germany. I figured I'd be there a year, and then they'd send me to 'Nam, but I stayed there in Germany the whole time."

When he got out, Carlisle's first thought was the oil business, but the timing wasn't quite right.

"The summer that I got out of high school [1959], my family moved to McComb, Mississippi, where my father went to work with my uncle in the oil business," he says. "So I thought about that, but it was kind of in the doldrums at the time, so I spent five years in the investment banking business in New York and Dallas.

"But when they had the first oil embargo in 1973, prices went up, activity went up, and it was a good time to jump in. So I moved to McComb—my wife's hometown—and went to work with my father-in-law. I've been in the oil and gas business ever since.

"I met a geologist named Riley Hagan, and we became partners and did a lot of work together over a lot of years, drilled a lot of wells, made a lot of money. But of course, it got really crazy during the boom starting in the 1970s. When the bust hit in the 1980s, it affected the oil business, the real estate business, and the banking business, and a lot of people went down—got out.

"We survived, but eventually moved into just buying and selling, and that's what I'm doing now. Riley died a few years ago, but one of the projects we worked on for years is coming to fruition now, and it will be very good for me and Riley's widow. And I'm working on another project with about the same kind of lead time.

"In fact, I think the next four or five years will be the best I've ever had in the oil business. I'm 63 and still working hard, but I'm enjoying it."

Carlisle and his wife, Emily, have been married for 40 years and have two daughters: Kathy, 36, who lives in Atlanta, and Eloise, 32, who lives in Austin.

"We have six grandchildren," Carlisle says. "Up until recently, they had produced five girls, which I actually prefer, but the youngest just came up with a little boy, so we need to work him into the mix."

Overall, he says, it is a life of satisfaction and contentment.

"I grew up in a great place," he says. "Back then, Athens was a nice, friendly town with about 10,000 people. McComb is about the same size and the same kind of place.

"I've come full circle."

Where Have You Gone?

RAYMOND CLAYBORN

G lancing back over his 15-year career in the National Football League, Raymond Clayborn is struck by the irony.

"All the time I was a kid, growing up in Fort Worth," he says, "I loved the Dallas Cowboys. Especially Bob Hayes—'The Bullet.'

"I know that to kids today, Emmitt [Smith] is the famous No. 22—and he should be. But to me, No. 22 has always meant Bob Hayes.

"My mom used to take me over to the Cotton Bowl to watch the Cowboys play, and it was my biggest thrill. Or on Sunday mornings, I'd be glued to the TV, watching *The Tom Landry Show*, waiting for the game to start. Even after I started playing pro ball, I pulled for them to win except when I was playing against them."

Then years later, Clayborn suffered a career-ending injury against—the Cowboys. So much for rewarding faithful fans.

"It was an ankle injury," he says, laughing, "and after 15 years that was about it. It was my last game. By that time, I wasn't enjoying it that much anyway."

Such was not always the case, however.

When Clayborn was selected by New England in the first round of the 1977 draft, it was the achievement of a dream come true—a beginning to the career he had dreamed of since he was seven years old.

When he walked away in 1991, he closed a career—13 seasons with the Patriots and two with Cleveland—that included three All-Pro years and a Super Bowl appearance. At one point, he had also set a New England franchise record (since broken) with 36 career interceptions.

"For about the first 12 years, I loved it," he says. "But of course, as I grew older it became harder to do the training, harder to get up for the games. You're playing a kids' game, and you have to have that kind of enthusiasm to do it well. You have to be enthused and determined to be the best. Eventually, it begins to fade.

"Somewhere in there, I guess it dawned on me, 'Wow! I don't really love doing this anymore.' You eventually realize that it's a business, and you're just getting up

RAYMOND CLAYBORN
Hgt: 6-1 • Wgt: 190 • Hometown: Fort Worth

Years played: 1973-1976
Positions: Defensive back
Highlights: 1975: All-SWC; 1976: All-SWC, All-American

every day and going to work at your job. After that, you're getting older and your attitude is getting worse.

"I enjoyed college ball a lot more, and I began to long for the atmosphere of the college game."

In 1985, Clayborn played on an ill-fated Super Bowl team with New England. After beating the Dolphins for the AFC title—and their first win at the Orange Bowl in 18 years—the Patriots were trounced by the Bears 46-10 in the Super Bowl.

"I was the MVP of that Miami game," he says, "but in the Super Bowl I don't recall them throwing a single ball in my direction, not that it mattered, since they were beating us so bad."

Then into his all-pro years, Clayborn had encountered a common peril among highly regarded cornerbacks.

"I got most of my interceptions in the first six years, when we had Mike Haynes at the other corner," he says. "After he left, I can remember a lot of games over the years where nobody threw in my direction. That also took some of the fun out of it."

"But as far as looking back on my career, an overall view—I'd have to say I had a ball," he says. "I was out there for years making a lot of money playing a kids' game. I really have no complaints."

Few have ever had complaints about Clayborn's talent, but there has been something akin to mass confusion. Coming up through Fort Worth's Trimble Tech High School and later at Texas, he was almost too gifted for his own good.

"When I was in high school, we usually didn't have a lot of good players, so I kind of got moved around," he says. "Whenever we had someone who could throw the ball out there, I played wide receiver. When we didn't, I moved into the backfield to run the ball. Sometimes we didn't even have anybody who could hand the ball off, so I played quarterback. And I always played on defense in the secondary."

This was followed by a rather unusual recruiting process.

"Not many people knew about me, so I didn't get recruited by any big schools," he says. "I was all set to go to West Texas State, because they were about the only school recruiting me. They even flew me out there for a visit, the first time I was ever on a plane. I wasn't real crazy about the place, but that's where I was going.

"Then one day a Texas recruiter, Timmy Doerr, showed up. He told me he had been recruiting several players in the area, and he said, 'Every time I'm looking at game film on some guy we're recruiting—you show up on the film. Finally I started asking, "Who *is* this guy?" And they'd say, "Probably the best player in the city."'

"I was running track and told him I couldn't visit right away. By the time I visited down there, they were in spring drills. But they held a scholarship for me."

At Texas, Clayborn continued to shuffle among several positions.

"When I first got there, they said they wanted me at running back, so I played there some as a freshman. Then they brought in Earl Campbell and Alfred Jackson, so they were going to use me as a wide receiver my sophomore year.

"But we opened against some teams that threw the ball a lot, so they moved me to the secondary and told me they would move me back to receiver later in the season.

"Then they said the pros were interested in me as a defensive back and that's where they wanted to see me. And I said, 'If that's where they want to see me, that's where I'll be.'"

He ended his career as an All-American and first-round draft pick.

In the years since he left the NFL, Clayborn has been involved in a variety of pursuits, including one involving his old teammate Earl Campbell.

"For the first couple of years I just took it easy and did basically nothing," he says. "Then I got a divorce and figured it was time to go back to work.

"That's when I ran into Earl. He and Merv Griffin and Sidney Poitier were involved in a casino—Players' Casino—in Lake Charles, and they offered me a job. Basically they wanted me to just come over on the weekends and greet people, like the club celebs they have in Las Vegas and Atlantic City.

"So I would go back and forth between Houston and Lake Charles on the weekends. Houston was also a target area for them to find people to come over and gamble, so I was doing that, too. They called it player development.

"Merv and Earl would come down about once a month, and that went on for about five or six years. But then Merv got prostate cancer, and his girlfriend, Eva Gabor, died, and he pulled out."

By that time, Clayborn had remarried. He and his wife, Kimberly, have been married 10 years and have two children: a girl, Sydney, 9, and a boy, R.J. (Raymond Jr.), 5.

He now works for the state comptroller in a variety of roles and also works with the NFL, monitoring the Texans in a uniform compliance role.

"I have no complaints," says Clayborn, who recently turned 50. "I've had a good life, and I'm looking for 50 more years.

"Besides, if I did have something to complain about, most folks wouldn't listen because they've got their own problems."

Where Have You Gone?

JACK COLLINS

When the time came for Jack Collins to choose the ultimate path that his life would follow, it is safe to say that his selection method was a little wobbly.

"When I had one semester left at UT, I got drafted by Pittsburgh," he says. "So I signed for $3,000—which seemed like a lot of money—went to training camp with them, and got cut. I spent the rest of the season with the Dallas Cowboys on the taxi squad, and when the season was over, I came back down here and finished my degree.

"The next year I went back to training camp with the Cowboys, but it didn't look like things were working out, and I got discouraged. This would have been in 1962, and we got slaughtered in an exhibition game by the Green Bay Packers, and I never even got into the game.

"The next day we had to go back out to Thousand Oaks to training camp, and when I was sitting on the plane waiting to take off, something hit me all of a sudden—

"And it said, 'You probably ought to go do something else.'

"I got off and saw coach [Tom] Landry and told him I was leaving, and he said, 'Oh no, don't do that. You'll get a chance—if not here, I'll try to get you placed somewhere else.'

"I told him thanks anyway, but I was sure about it, and walked off. My bags and all my clothes went to California and I never saw 'em again."

And that is how Collins set in motion a 40-year career in the banking business.

"I enrolled for a semester at SMU," he says, "and met some people from Republic Bank in Dallas and went to work there in January of 1964. I had a business degree, and originally I thought that if I went to work in banking, I might eventually find something I really wanted to do. I've been in it ever since."

It was an easy transition for Collins and his wife, Nancy, who both grew up in Dallas and have known each other since high school.

JACK COLLINS
Hgt: 6-0 • Wgt: 190 • Hometown: Dallas

Years played: 1959-1961
Positions: Halfback, flanker, defensive back
Highlights: 1959: All-SWC; led team in rushing, receiving, total offense,
all-purpose yards, and punting; scored winning touchdown in the 1962
Cotton Bowl

"We knew each other at Highland Park and then went to Texas together," he says. "We didn't date all that time, but we got married in 1962, and we've been together ever since.

"Actually, we had just gotten married when I had to report to training camp with Pittsburgh, so she went with me. The team moved to a site in West Virginia, so she stayed with friends in Pittsburgh and came over to visit me on weekends.

"It was great planning on my part. We'd been married for two weeks, and I was having to sneak out of the dorm to meet her for a date."

Collins worked for Republic Bank for 10 years, and then he and Nancy moved back to Austin in 1974. Their two children—Allison, 39, and Burke, 36—both live in Florida.

"We've been back here for 30 years," says Collins, now with Frost Bank in Austin, "and neither of us has any family left in Dallas. So we're here to stay."

It has been a good life. Which is not to say that there has never been a twinge of regret.

"Growing up, it had always been my dream to play pro ball," he says. "It was hard to let go. It really was hard, and it haunted me for years.

"Not having a good experience in pro ball bothered me for a long time. It was the first time in my life I felt like I had been fired from a job. The first time I felt that I had failed.

"For a long time, I kind of played the what if game—what if I had tried to play in Canada or maybe tried my luck with an AFL team. I always wondered. But eventually, as the years pass, it kind of fades away."

The sense of loss is understandable. As a senior at Highland Park, he led the Scots to the 1957 Class 4-A state title, averaging 9.3 yards per carry while rushing for 1,480 yards and scoring 161 points. Along the way, he became the hero of one of the most famous games in Texas schoolboy history.

It came in the state semifinals, played in the Cotton Bowl, when the Scots played Chuck Moser's legendary Abilene Eagles, who had won three straight state championships and were rolling toward a fourth. During that span they had won 49 straight games and had been featured in *Life* magazine.

The previous week they had demolished unbeaten Amarillo 33-14 and were 14-point favorites over the Scots. But a memorable battle unfolded, and with 3:36 remaining and the Scots trailing 20-14, lightning struck.

Quarterback Bobby Reed threw a long pass to Collins, who caught it at the Abilene 36 and raced in for the score, completing a 58-yard play. He then kicked the extra point, but the Scots drew a 15-yard penalty and he missed the second try.

The game ended in a 20-20 tie, and with a 5-3 edge in penetrations, Highland Park advanced to the title game, and Abilene's streak was broken. The following week, the Scots beat Port Arthur for the title.

"At the time, I didn't even know what a penetration was," Collins says, laughing. "I was just glad that there was such a thing.

"To this day, I can remember that when Tugboat Jones came to Highland Park to be our coach, he said he was looking for a team that could beat Abilene. And we had actually done it."

Widely recruited, Collins chose Texas. During his three-year career, the Longhorns played four games in the Cotton Bowl—two against SMU and two in the Cotton Bowl game.

"Every time we played in that stadium," he says, "I remembered that Abilene game. I would walk over to that spot where I caught that pass and just stand there for a minute."

As a sophomore in 1959, Collins led the Longhorns in rushing, receiving, and total offense and was an All-SWC selection on a 9-1 team that went to the Cotton Bowl, where it fell to Syracuse's national champions 23-14.

Collins caught a 69-yard touchdown pass from Bobby Lackey but points out that earlier, "Syracuse also threw a long touchdown pass—right over me and Lackey."

In 1960, Collins was featured on the cover of the inaugural issue of Dave Campbell's *Texas Football Magazine*. Then he got hurt.

"The old magazine cover jinx," he says, laughing. "It was all downhill from there. As far as that season goes, I missed most of it.

"It started off when I pulled a hamstring before the season started. Then when I did try to play, I hurt a knee. I played in about half the games, basically operating on one leg."

As a senior he was moved to wingback in the new Wing-T formation and was used primarily as a wide receiver and lead blocker for James Saxton on the power sweep. In his final game, he caught a 24-yard pass for the winning touchdown in the Cotton Bowl game against Ole Miss.

As the years have passed Collins has grown comfortable in the role of successful banker and leading citizen—he has been active in United Way and served as president of the Boy Scouts and director of the Chamber of Commerce, among other activities. Some memories have faded; some haven't.

"That Abilene game still stands out as a highlight," he says, "along with some of the experiences I had in college. But the main thing is that sports has just always been a big part of my life—and it has brought me so many positive experiences.

"I know people who had a bad experience with their high school coaches, or something similar, but I didn't. I had good experiences, and in both high school and college I didn't have to play on a team that never won.

"It was a very enjoyable part of my life, and I think a lot of it rubs off in other things that you do. It builds confidence and has played a role in many of the friendships that I've developed."

In fact, it is not clear that Collins—who at 64 is in excellent shape—could be called a "former" athlete.

"My father-in-law was a cardiologist and got me real interested in exercise as a health issue," he says. "I started jogging when I was 25, but for about 30 years now I've also been doing some kind of aerobic exercise.

"My dad [whose 95-yard interception return against Baylor in 1936 is still a UT record] had a heart attack when he was 53. Another one killed him when he was 60. His dad died of one when he was in his 40s. So it seemed like a good idea for me to be concerned about my health.

"When I was 54, I ran a marathon at White Rock Lake in Dallas. It was a big accomplishment for me, but I've had two knee surgeries since then, so I think it was the last one.

"Overall, I feel very fortunate for the opportunities I've had in life—the way I grew up, my family, a successful career in banking. I'm looking forward to another 25 years."

At this point, Collins can think of only one really big problem: his kids.

"Allison is married to a plastic surgeon in Vero Beach and has three boys; Burke has a physical rehab business in Tampa and has three girls," he says.

"The whole lot of 'em are Gator fans."

Where Have You Gone?

MIKE COTTEN

E ach year, Mike Cotten takes a brief timeout from his busy schedule with the Austin law firm of Clark, Thomas, and Winters to attend a reunion of his old football team.

Not the Texas Longhorns—the Quantico Marines.

It's a team he played for in 1964 and 1965, prior to being shipped overseas for a tour in Vietnam. The reunions, he says, began about three years ago.

"Basically, a bunch of guys who hadn't seen each other in 35 years," he says, "but shared a common bond. It's become an enjoyable, and important, annual event for us."

Not that Cotten has abandoned the Longhorns, with whom he had a memorable career (1959-1961) as a quarterback and defensive back.

A star quarterback at Austin High who once lived a block away from Darrell Royal, he grew up with no doubts about where he wanted to go to college. When his playing career at UT was done, he served for two years as a graduate assistant while finishing his law degree.

In 1968, when his tour of duty with the Marines was over, he returned home and went to work for the law firm. He has worked there ever since.

His wife, Betty, whom he met at UT, has worked with the Texas Exes for the last 15 years, arranging trips to various parts of the world, and the Cottens often take vacation trips with the Exes.

He still goes to the games, and in many respects is a typical Texas Ex and fan.

But once, long ago, like thousands of other American youths of the era, he went through an experience that has never disappeared from the memory and forged lasting bonds between men who otherwise would have been total strangers.

"I decided in high school that I wanted to be an officer," he says, "and that I wanted to be a Marine officer.

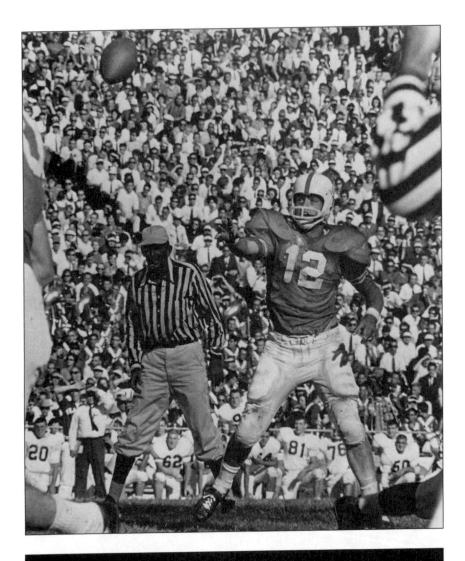

MIKE COTTEN
Hgt: 6-0 • Wgt: 190 • Hometown: Austin

Years played: 1959-1961
Positions: Quarterback, defensive back
Highlights: Led team to a No. 3 national ranking as
starting quarterback in 1961

"I wasn't looking for a career in the military, but I definitely planned to do my duty and serve my time [in the era of the universal draft], and I had the commitment to do it. I began studying for it in high school.

"I got my commission when I graduated from Texas, but they deferred me for two years to finish law school. Then I was sent to Quantico for what is called The Basic School.

"Quantico still fielded football teams in those days, and there were always a lot of former college players in school there, including guys from West Point and Annapolis. But we never received any special treatment—we went through the Marine training and played football in our extra time. That rule was the same for everybody."

Of course, service ball differed slightly from the pure collegiate variety, Cotten recalls.

"After the games, everybody would go somewhere and light up a cigarette and start drinking beer," he says, laughing. "In fact, some guys would be smoking cigarettes at halftime.

"But we had a lot of fun. In the last game of the 1965 season, we beat Memphis State and knocked them out of the Liberty Bowl. It was such a big deal that we actually made the scores in the paper the next day."

After that, Cotten went overseas and wound up at Da Nang.

"I was in a legal billet," he says. "We took rocket fire a few times when the air base was attacked, but I was never a combatant. But I was proud to be there.

"I had planned to do military service because I felt it was my duty, and the war just happened to be going on when I did it. I went gladly, and I would do it again, because—that was just what you did.

"Looking back on it now, of course, I know things I didn't know then. We made some mistakes that I hope we learned from.

"The main thing you learned after you got there was that the people weren't necessarily on our side. You thought you were there to help them fight and that they would fight on your side, but it didn't work that way.

"The people out in the villages were really very far removed from the government in Saigon. So whoever was in town that day—the Viet Cong or the Marines—that's the side they were on. But I was glad that I went."

For the next three decades, Cotten had little or no contact with the men he had known at Quantico. Then a few years ago, the reunions coalesced around a particular quest: to find the grave of Tommy Holden.

"It's kind of an amazing story," Cotten says. "Tommy was a kid from New Jersey who played on those 1964 and 1965 teams at Quantico. That's where I met him.

"He was a linebacker—a tough kid who had come out of the Naval Academy. In fact, he was on the 1963 Navy team with Roger Staubach that played against Texas in the Cotton Bowl.

"In October of 1966, he was killed in action."

In his brief time in Vietnam, Holden won two Silver Stars and two Purple Hearts. His body was sent home for burial, but as the years rolled by and his family members either died or moved away, the location of his grave was lost to his former comrades.

"Finally," Cotten says, "a couple of the guys started looking for Tommy's grave. One of them, Gene Carrington, a big tackle from Boston College, eventually wrote a story about it."

Carrington, a particularly close friend, had visited Holden (they were in different units) shortly before he was killed. When he came back and started a family, he named his son Thomas James Holden Carrington. For years, his daughter wore a yellow Marine T-shirt that had belonged to Holden to bed every night. He kept a picture of Holden on his desk.

He had visited Holden's parents upon his return from Vietnam, but they were still so heartbroken over the loss that he decided not to go back. When he retired from Exxon in 1997 and planned a pilgrimage to his friend's grave, he discovered that Holden had not been buried in his hometown. Records had vanished, newspaper accounts did not mention a burial site, and no relatives could be located.

Over the next few years, Carrington contacted former members of the Quantico group, found more reliable newspaper accounts, and finally located Holden's cousin, who told him where the grave was. By that time, word had spread to Holden's former Naval Academy classmates.

Finally, on a March day in 2001, a total of 30 people—including a Marine honor guard—converged on St. Mary's Cemetery in Bangall, New York, and made their way to Holden's grave. Carrington had difficulty speaking. Friends and relatives wept. A rifle salute was fired. The bugler played "Taps."

When it was over, the sergeant in charge of the honor guard, tears in his eyes, told Carrington that the most inspiring thing he had ever seen was that so many people had come so far, after all those years, to pay homage to a fallen comrade.

"After all that time," Cotten says, "Tommy brought us all back together again. Now we have the reunion every year in his honor, and it means a lot to us all."

As for his *other* team, he says, "Growing up here, I had always wanted to go to UT, and when Coach Royal came in and turned the program around during my senior year in high school, that was a positive sign. Bobby Nunis and I made our announcement on the first day of recruiting, and I never visited another campus.

"In those days we lived at 1302 Belmont Parkway, and Coach Royal lived in the next block, but I hardly ever saw him.

"I was playing football and baseball at Austin High, and we had good teams. We reached the semifinals in football and won the state championship in baseball, here in Austin.

"After the game, about 10 p.m., Nunis and I met Mike Campbell at Hill's Steakhouse and had a big steak and signed our letters of intent. Then I got into a friend of mine's 1958 Impala, and we drove nonstop to Gallup, New Mexico, where

I had a summer job with Western Pipeline. I worked for them on the pipeline for all or part of the next seven summers."

During his playing career, Cotten became part of the group that emphatically stamped the Royal era as a burgeoning success story: a group that went 26-6-1, capped by a 10-1 season in 1961 ending with a 12-7 win over powerful Ole Miss in the Cotton Bowl.

In the process, he also became the quarterback of Royal's first great offensive innovation: Long before the Wishbone, there was the Flip Flop—an innovative Wing-T attack that befuddled the opposition in almost every instance.

Mike Cotten (*Photo courtesy of the Cotten family*)

In nine regular-season victories that year, Texas averaged better than 32 points per game. The lone exception was a 6-0 upset loss to TCU at a point when the Longhorns were ranked No. 1 in the nation.

"Just a horrible game," Cotten says, "and naturally, there has been more said and written about it than any of the victories. We had some injuries and some bad luck, but TCU also was a tough team with some good players, and by that time—the ninth game of the season—they were well prepared to stop the power sweep we had run so often."

As Cotten progressed through college, his interest in law and government increased, and after graduation he received a two-year deferment to finish law school before reporting to Quantico. He has now been a practicing attorney for more than 35 years, with the same firm.

"We have a pretty broad civil practice," he says. "We do a good bit of regulatory work, state agency work, banking law, products liabilities—it involves about 100 some-odd lawyers, overall."

He and his wife, the former Betty George, have been married for 40 years and have two daughters—Ashley, 34, who lives in Austin and has three children; and Lesley, 30, who lives in Jackson, Mississippi, and has two children.

"In recent years," he says, "many of our most enjoyable moments have been connected with my wife's job with the Texas Exes. She's the travel agent for the Flying Longhorns, which involves about 30 to 35 trips a year for games, tours, and so forth. We've taken several vacations to spots around the world.

"Last summer we went to Russia—St. Petersburg and Moscow and a trip down the rivers. It's a very interesting country, especially if you know the history of it.

"We've also gone to China—Beijing, the Great Wall, Xi-An, where they have the 2,000 terra cotta warriors—and a three-day boat ride down the Yangtse River. We went through the Three Gorges before they were flooded for the new industrial project, and it was an amazing trip.

"After that we went on to Shanghai and Hong Kong, but that's more like going to New York.

"I also took a trip to Thailand and Singapore—but I've never gone back to Vietnam.

"You can always look back and see things you would do differently. But I've been blessed in my family and professional life, and had great experiences in athletics. I don't know how I could ask for anything more."

Where Have You Gone?

GIB DAWSON

Completing a recent medical checkup, Gib Dawson was told by his doctor that he seems in remarkably good health, "for someone your age."

It cheered Dawson up some. After all, it's kind of a nice thing to say to a guy who's 74.

Nevertheless, Dawson, a retiree who owns homes in both Phoenix and Tucson, seems committed to living a dangerous life.

"Last year before Christmas," he says, "I was at home here [in Phoenix] trying to put up a home entertainment center, and the dang thing fell over on top of me.

"It collapsed one of my kidneys, and I had a real problem with it and wound up in the hospital. They said the kidney was doing about two percent of what it's supposed to, and I lost about 15 pounds. In fact, I nearly died. But they finally got it all squared away, and I'm okay now.

"But I think that thing weighed about 500 pounds, and I have to be a little more careful at my age. So I just don't mess with crap like that anymore—I'll call and have someone else do it."

Recovered from injury and returned to the sanctity of his domicile, Dawson was then attacked from behind by a creature known as The Duke of Marlette.

"He's my pet Doberman," Dawson says. "I named him Duke, and the street we live on is Marlette, so that's what I call him. Anyway, I was fixing his food one day, and that gets him excited, and as I was carrying it to the back for him, he rushed up and jumped on me from behind.

"I'll tell you, I don't think I ever got hit that hard playing football. He weighs close to 150, and I went flying, and dog food went flying all over the place, and I wound up at the doctor's again. He thinks I may have torn a little cartilage, and I'm walking with a cane, but it's slowly getting better."

It has usually been an event-filled life for Dawson, who came out of Douglas, Arizona, as a nationally recruited running back, became a star at the University of Texas, and played briefly with Green Bay before being called up in the Army.

GIB DAWSON
Hgt: 5-11 • Wgt: 176 • Hometown: Douglas, Arizona

Years played: 1950-1952
Position: Halfback
Highlights: All-SWC in 1952;
ranks 16th on all-time UT rushing list with 1,724 yards

By the time he got out it was nearly three years later and a pro football career was beginning to recede into the past. He went back to Arizona, got married, raised a family, and got into the wholesale liquor business. He retired twice and did well enough to build a comfortable life.

Somewhere along the way, he seems to have dodged a bullet. His father and younger brother both died of sudden heart attacks at age 41, but if there is a hereditary strain there, Dawson escaped it.

But life, as they say, is a great leveler. No one dodges every bullet, and the one that hit Dawson a few years ago left a big hole.

"In 2003, I lost my wife, Marion, to cancer," he says. "We were married 48 years, and I'm having a real hard time coping with it.

"I'm still living here in the house, but it's a pretty big place for just me and the dog. I have another house down in Tucson, but I don't know if I want to go down there.

"But walking around here—every time I turn around, there's something that reminds me of Marion. We were very close, not just as husband and wife, but as good friends. We loved to travel, and we traveled all over the world together.

"I met her on a plane—back then she was a flight attendant for American Airlines, and in less than six months we were married. Now, I'm having a real tough time with this.

"She was a great lady. I'm just sitting around trying to figure out what to do next."

For many years, there always seemed no shortage of people with suggestions on what Dawson should do next.

"When I was growing up, we lived in Douglas," he says. "My dad—he was Gilbert, and I was Gilbert Jr.—dabbled in the cattle business a little bit and had a little bar called Dawson's Tavern.

"I had a big high school career, and I guess I was recruited by just about every major school in the country. I must have had about 100 offers.

"I kind of had it down to Texas or Oklahoma, and I was kind of leaning toward OU. But my dad had grown up in Monahans and wanted me to go to Texas, so I did.

"It wasn't always easy. I was the only guy on the team who wasn't from Texas, and it was kind of like being a Yankee. For a while I had a hard time fitting in, and I called my dad several times and told him I was coming home, but he talked me out of it.

"I'm not sure I was really accepted until my senior year, but they put me in the Hall of Honor years later, so I guess I came out okay."

As a sophomore in 1950, Dawson played on a championship team—the last one coached by Blair Cherry.

"He was a very stern, no-nonsense-type guy, and his offense was geared toward making first downs," Dawson says. "A 15-yard run was a big gain.

"We lost to Oklahoma by one point, and it was the third straight loss to them, and the alums never let him forget it. I think it cost him his job.

"We lost to Tennessee 20-14 in the Cotton Bowl. I was the idiot that fumbled the ball at our 43 late in the game that led to their winning touchdown."

The next year, under Ed Price, the Longhorns beat Oklahoma. But it was, up to that time, the worst day of Dawson's life.

"It was the day my dad died," he says. "He was there in Dallas and died the morning of the game. I would always send tickets home, and he would come, or the family would. That day, my mom and brother were also there.

"I was already dressed and taped for the game. I was sitting there, talking to him, when it happened. Just all of a sudden—with no warning—he had a heart attack. There had never been a history of it in the family as far as we knew. It was just such a shock—sitting there talking, and then he's gone.

"Mr. Cherry—Blair's brother—kind of stepped in and took charge. They took us to the hospital, then the airport, and within an hour we were on Mr. Cherry's private plane flying back to Arizona. It was all just—unbelievable.

"But years later, my brother died—in his sleep—at the same age."

Returning to the team the next week, Dawson finished the season as the team's leading rusher and averaged 7.1 yards per carry, culminating with a 158-yard performance against Texas A&M. But Texas lost that one, 22-21, for its third defeat, which added up to a disappointing season.

By this time, Price had changed the offense to a Split-T option attack—a forerunner of the Wishbone—and the 1952 Longhorns won the SWC title. They also came up with an amazing achievement: Every man in the backfield—Dawson, T Jones, Dick Ochoa, and Billy Quinn—was named All-Conference.

"It was amazing," Dawson says. "I don't recall ever hearing of another instance where an entire All-Conference backfield came from one school."

One game became a disaster—a 49-20 loss to a superb Oklahoma team. But Dawson believes it was partly a result of a 14-3 loss to Notre Dame the previous week.

"We should have won that game," he says. "Physically, we beat the crap out of them. It was really hot that day, and by the end of the game they could barely walk back to the dressing room. They didn't belong on the same field with us.

"But we gave them an easy touchdown by fumbling a punt near our goal line, and we fumbled again going in at their goal line, and that's a 14-point swing. We drove down three or four times and only got a field goal [kicked by Dawson].

"We were still down from that the next week. OU was a great team, but we were down by 21 points in the first quarter before we finally woke up."

From there, the Longhorns recovered and rolled to a 9-2 finish, including a 16-0 victory over Tennessee in the Cotton Bowl. The score hardly indicated UT's dominance that day, as the Longhorns finished with 301 total yards to 32 for the Vols.

Gib Dawson and his wife, Marion, with their grandchildren: (standing) Travis, Taylor, Coleton; (sitting) Lauren and Mark (*Photo courtesy of the Dawson family*)

"After the Oklahoma game, we just kept getting stronger," Dawson says. "I really believe that by the time we played Tennessee, we were as good as any team in the country. I was proud to end my career that way."

He finished with 1,724 career yards, still good for 16th on the all-time list at UT.

After leaving Texas, Dawson had a pro career that was a bit short and an Army career that was a little long.

"I played with Green Bay in 1953," he says, "and I probably wouldn't have made any money at all if it hadn't been for Doak Walker and Bobby Layne, who were with Detroit at the time.

"They gave me some advice about negotiating a contract. They also had a plan to get me over to Detroit in a trade, but I was the MVP in the All-Star Game, and Green Bay wouldn't trade me.

"Didn't really matter, because that was the only year I played. I got a commission coming out of college, and the Army took me after that first season, because so many officers were getting killed over in Korea and they needed more.

"It was supposed to be two years, but they extended me another six months, which basically made it three years out of football. By the time I got out, my wife was expecting a child, and I finally decided just to stay in Arizona and go to work.

"Funny deal: When Marion and I met, she didn't know anything about me playing football. But she had already met Bobby Layne and Harley Sewell because she flew out of Detroit as a home base and they were with the Lions. She and Harley lived in the same apartment building.

"Anyway, I talked to Bobby Dillon about it—he was with the Packers then—and he told me I was good enough to come back because I could kick and play defense as well as run. I even talked to Vince Lombardi on the phone a couple of times after he became the coach.

"But I ended up going into the wholesale liquor business with a man here in Phoenix. I guess maybe I missed football a little, but to tell you the truth, so many guys I knew came out of that game all banged up and beaten up, and a lot of them are dead now. So I probably don't really regret it.

"There are so many of those old guys who basically built pro football into what it is, and now they're old and sick and can't pay medical bills and the NFL, with all its money, won't do anything to help them. It's a shame."

For Dawson, it turned out to be a good choice.

"I worked in the liquor business for about 18 years and did really well, and then I retired and didn't do anything for a couple of years. Then I met a guy who was chairman of the board with Circle K Corporation, and I met with them, and they talked me into coming out of retirement to set up all their liquor operations.

"I did that for nearly 10 years. It was supposed to be a three-day-a-week job, but it turned into seven days a week and 14-hour days, so I finally said that's it and retired again.

"I had a pretty good life, not doing too much. I had a house over on the coast, but I gave that to the kids. Our kids were grown and getting on with their own lives."

Dawson's two sons live in Phoenix—Gilbert III is in the trucking business, and Glenn runs a large wholesale beer warehouse.

His daughter, Carolyn Stymiest, lives in Dallas and is a senior executive vice president with Blue Cross/Blue Shield.

"I used to play golf a lot," he says. "Miller Barber and Don January used to come out here, and I would play with them."

He quit playing golf when Marion got sick.

"That disease is such a horrible thing," he says. "We tried everything and every doctor or clinic you could think of, but once it started, there was nothing anyone could do. The last year was just terrible.

"So now I'm kind of rattling around in this big house, me and the dog. I used to have another one that was kind of tan, like a steer, so I called him Bevo. This one's black, and he's pretty spoiled. He sleeps in the bed with me. I mean, I have my side and he has his. Puts his head on the pillow. It's ridiculous.

"I've got the house in Tucson, but it's three stories and built on the side of a mountain, so there's a lot of stairs, and I don't think that's what I need. This one has four bedrooms and a guest house and a pool and palm trees and fruit trees and a big backyard, and it's more than I need. So I'm just trying to make some decisions.

"I may start playing golf again—if I can stay out of the way of that damn dog."

Where Have You Gone?

CHRIS GILBERT

When Chris Gilbert played his first football game at the University of Texas, John Wayne was standing on the opposite sideline.

This, however, was not quite as ominous as it may sound. "The Duke" was not there to command the opposing forces. He was simply a large fan (and alum) of USC, the team the Longhorns were playing.

"I was just a sophomore, sitting on the bench in the season opener," Gilbert says. "Suddenly, coach [Darrell] Royal decides to send me in with a play, on which I'm supposed to carry the ball. It was about the second quarter, and we were behind and didn't seem to be doing too well, so I guess he just wanted to change something.

"So I go in and carry the ball, and the play works and we gain some yards. So another signal comes in from the bench saying run the same play, and we do it again and gain some more yards. They send in another signal saying run it again to the opposite side. So it works again.

"So they run it again for a fourth time and a fifth time, and I'm gaining yards and getting more pumped up each time, and the team and the fans are getting pumped up, and I'm just going crazy.

"Finally, I got so excited that I started hyperventilating, and they had to take me out of the game."

An interesting beginning, to say the least, for a career that eventually earned Gilbert a place in the National Football Foundation Hall of Fame.

From 1966 to 1968, he became the first player in NCAA history to rush for 1,000 yards or more in each of his eligible seasons (freshmen were ineligible at the time). He topped 100 yards in exactly half of his 32 games, had four games of 200-plus yards, was an All-American and the leading rusher on the first Wishbone team in Texas history, and had a 96-yard touchdown run that is still a UT standard.

His 3,231 career yards—a school record at the time—still rank fourth after nearly four decades behind Ricky Williams, Cedric Benson, and Earl Campbell.

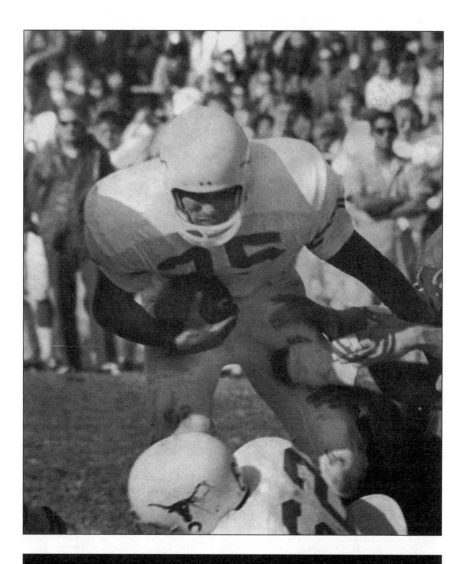

CHRIS GILBERT
Hgt: 5-11 • Wgt: 176 • Hometown: Houston

Years played: 1966-1968
Position: Running back
Highlights: 1966: All-SWC, leading rusher; 1967: All-SWC, leading
rusher; 1968: All-SWC, Consensus All-American, leading rusher; finished
eighth in Heisman voting; ranks fourth on all-time UT rushing list with
3,231 yards; ranks third on list of 100-yard games with 16; first player
in NCAA history to rush for more than 1,000 yards
in each season of eligibility

But for Gilbert, who has built a successful Houston real estate business over the past 35 years, the legacy of his career at UT is not to be found on any personal stat sheet.

"My first two seasons there were very frustrating," he says, "because we went 6-4 both years. We had good players, and all the losses were close, by a touchdown or less.

"You always had the feeling that with a couple of breaks it could have been a successful season, and that made it more frustrating. We had all come to Texas to win championships, and it wasn't happening, and that was very troubling."

Prior to Gilbert's senior year, however, a mad scientist named Emory Bellard invented the Wishbone offense. With a few adjustments following an opening tie and a loss, the thing jelled and began rolling down the road, flattening everything in sight.

The Longhorns finished the 1968 season with nine straight wins, a Southwest Conference championship, a 36-13 rout of Tennessee in the Cotton Bowl, and a No. 3 national ranking. It was the beginning of a run that included 30 wins in a row, six straight Cotton Bowl appearances, and two national championships.

The fact that he was gone by the time the 1969 team won a clear-cut national title has never bothered him, Gilbert says.

"To begin with," he says, "when we walked off the field at the Cotton Bowl after the Tennessee game, I felt like I was playing on the best team in America. We'd had a loss and a tie, but that was in the first two weeks. By the end of the season, we were as good as anyone out there.

"In fact, Steve Kiner, an All-American on that Tennessee team, later told me that they were totally unprepared for what they ran into that day, that they had no idea how to stop it, and that from early in the game they knew it was a no-win situation. We were still running in new plays no one had ever seen before.

"But the main thing is that a momentum change in a program can be an awesome thing to see, and that's what we did. We were the first team of the Wishbone era, and we got that program back to winning championships. If you can ever be a part of that, it's such a big thing, so much more important than rushing records or scoring records. I will always be proud that I was a part of that."

Having been a Pop Warner All-American and an All-American at Spring Branch High School in Houston, Gilbert finished his career as a consensus All-American at Texas. He was drafted in the fourth round by the New York Jets.

But as Jets coach Weeb Ewbank soon discovered, Gilbert—who had grown up with a father and grandfather in the real estate business—was not a cheap date.

"I had people calling me from around the country wanting to represent me," he says, "but I decided to see if I could go up there and negotiate it myself, without an agent. Frank Denius, a successful businessman and UT supporter, gave me some valuable advice, and I went up to see Ewbank.

"There were a lot of Texas guys playing for the Jets, and I knew most weren't making that much. But when they had signed Joe Namath for $400,000, it made the front page of the papers, and I remembered that.

"I sat down with Weeb at his office in the stadium up there, and he handed me a contract with another guy's name on it but with the amount filled in. I think it was $22,000 to $23,000, something like that. I said, 'You've got the wrong guy.'

"And he said, 'No, that's what we paid our fourth-round choice last year, same contract.'

"I told him I wanted a no-cut contract for $40,000 for one year. I figured if I made it, I'd be worth more the next year, and if I didn't, I'd still have the money. He said that was way out of line, that I would be making more than 90 percent of the guys on the team, and I hadn't proven anything yet.

"I told him $40,000 was my number, so we never came close to making a deal. He called a couple of times after that, but I hadn't changed my mind."

This led Gilbert into the circle of beer baron Tommy Mercer, who owned the Fort Worth Braves of the Continental League.

"Tommy called me up, and I told him I had never heard of his team or the league," Gilbert says, "and besides, I was back in Austin trying to finish up my degree. And if I wouldn't play for the Jets for under $40,000—

"Amazingly, he came up with an offer I couldn't refuse. They had signed a TV deal, and he said he would put the money in the bank for me, that I could stay in Austin and just come up twice a week for workouts, that he would pay for the transportation and an apartment, and that I only had to play 50 percent of the time on offense in the games. So I signed.

"Pretty obviously, it was doomed from the start: I got special treatment, I worked out twice a week and never really had time to bond with my teammates, and they certainly weren't making the kind of money I was. It was an experience, but it wasn't all bad. I traveled around the country, and I actually enjoyed the season.

"I took the money I got from Tommy, invested it in a new bank starting up, and came out real well."

By that time, Gilbert and his college roommate, Corby Robertson, had partnered in something that would grow into a lifetime project: a summer camp on the north shore of Lake Livingston in East Texas.

Now known as Camp Olympia, it has been going strong for 35 years and has developed into a year-round facility with a full-time staff and a clientele ranging from such diverse locales as Europe and the Houston Independent School District.

"For both of us," Gilbert says, "it has been a labor of love."

It began as an idle thought at the end of the pair's junior year and grew quickly.

"We were sitting around talking about what we would do in the summer, and I said I would really like to start a boys' football camp," Gilbert says. "They didn't have football camps back then, but I had gone to a baseball camp as a kid and loved it.

"We kept talking about it, and his parents had some land they let us use, and we borrowed some money and built a couple of cabins. The next thing we knew, we had ourselves a football camp—not knowing the first thing about running one, of course. But back then it was not against the rules, so we went ahead.

"We always mentioned it whenever we were interviewed by the sportswriters, so we got a lot of free publicity. More and more kids started signing up, and we had to build more cabins, and it just went from there.

"Now we have a staff, and it's open to kids the year round. In the summers, the Houston ISD actually conducts some classes there, and we now have a large influx of kids coming in from Europe.

"I've had more enjoyment from this than you could ever imagine."

Also, a few years ago, Robertson built the highly acclaimed Whispering Pines golf course nearby, set up to benefit various medical charities.

Over the years, Gilbert has been highly successful in the real estate business and with a variety of investments.

"I guess it all started with that money I got from Tommy [Mercer]," he says, laughing. "I've just had good luck ever since with business decisions and investments."

Gilbert and his wife, Kim, have been married 34 years and have two sons.

"We met in high school, but we went off to different colleges," he says. "She went to Texas Tech and the University of Madrid, and we started dating when she came back from Spain."

One son, Chris, has had a life with as many twists and turns as his dad, beginning with the fact that one leg was amputated below the knee when he was 15.

"He was born with a congenital problem," Gilbert says. "His leg would break very easily between the knee and the ankle. If you looked at it on an X-ray, it looked like the middle of an hourglass. He broke his leg countless times, had numerous operations, had rods put in his leg, the whole thing.

"One of the most heartbreaking things was that he loved sports and being active, and there were so many things he wanted to do. The final straw came one day when, literally, he was walking along the beach and his leg broke.

"I talked to Leland Winston, a friend of mine who played football at Rice and is an orthopedic surgeon and the Rice team doctor. He suggested that Chris might be better off with a prosthesis, and that eventually he would be able to play golf, snow ski, and be much more active.

"So Chris made the decision himself and had the leg amputated. Since then he's been able to have a much more quality life. In fact, he satisfied his urge to be around sports by being one of the team trainers at Texas."

This soon led to a new phase in life.

"One day Chris was in the weight room," Gilbert says, "and all these guys wearing suits walked in. One of them was George Bush, who was still the governor at that time.

"So Chris struck up a conversation with him and learned that he had been looking for someplace fairly private to work out and decided the UT training room—part of a large entity drawing state funds—might be the perfect spot. He planned on working out Thursdays and Sundays.

"Then Chris said, 'Gee, I'm sorry, governor, the training room is closed on Sundays.'

"And Bush smiled at him and said, 'Not anymore.'"

In time, the relationship led to an accounting job in the governor's office for Gilbert's son, who had a business background. And when Bush launched his presidential campaign, Gilbert's son was added to the team.

"Throughout that whole first campaign, Chris was on the traveling team and went everywhere Bush went," Gilbert says. "He was the low man on the totem pole, doing whatever job was needed, but he was there. And for the next four years, throughout Bush's first term in the White House, Chris was in Washington as part of the operation.

"Then after working through the second campaign, Chris finally decided a few months ago to leave and get into the business world, and he's now in grad school at Rice. But it was quite an experience. He met a lot of people and traveled around the world."

The Gilberts' other son, Tom, is a laid-back Californian.

"He seems to change jobs more than I change socks," Gilbert says, laughing, "but basically he's just out there enjoying that California life.

"Sometimes, I'll get on a plane and go out there and enjoy it with him for a while. It ain't bad."

Where Have You Gone?

JERRY GRAY

Jerry Gray looks out his window and sees snow, which is pretty normal, because he's in Buffalo.

In a perfect world, Gray and his wife, Sherry—both from Lubbock—and their 13-year-old son, Jeremy, would probably prefer a more temperate climate.

But beyond that, Gray—the defensive coordinator for the Buffalo Bills—is right where he wants to be. And, he figures, pretty much on track, at 42, to achieve his goal of eventually becoming a head coach.

Ever since the days when he was a quarterback at Estacado High School in Lubbock, planning a future path and achieving goals have been among Gray's major strengths. As a result, everything he has ever done has been a success.

As a free safety at the University of Texas, he was a consensus All-American—twice—and a first-round pick in the NFL draft.

During a nine-year career as a cornerback with the Los Angeles Rams, Houston, and Tampa Bay, he was an All-Pro selection four times and a Pro Bowl MVP.

Progressing through a nine-year coaching career, he has been the defensive coordinator at Buffalo for four years. In each of the last two years, the Bills have had the top-ranked defense in the NFL.

And after roaming L.A. for years as a single pro football star, he married a home-town girl who knew his mother. They have been married 14 years, and he calls it, "the best decision I ever made."

Gray has been making good decisions since he carefully reviewed the qualifications of the colleges recruiting him out of Estacado.

"Well, I kind of got lost in the shuffle as far as Texas Tech was concerned, because they were going through a coaching change at the time," he says. "But that was never a problem, because I was getting recruited by a lot of high-profile schools—OU, Texas, several others. I looked at what each one had to offer and then picked Texas for two reasons.

"One was that I had decided that I wanted a career in the NFL if I was good enough, and I felt Texas gave me the best chance at that. I was being recruited basi-

JERRY GRAY

Hgt: 6-1 • Wgt: 183 • Hometown: Lubbock

Years played: 1981-1984
Position: Defensive back
Highlights: 1983: All-SWC, Consensus All-American; 1984:
All-SWC, Consensus All-American

cally as a defensive back, and switching from quarterback never bothered me because at that time, there wasn't much interest in minority quarterbacks in the NFL.

"At that time, Texas was really sending a lot of defensive backs to the NFL, probably more than any program in the country. Their man-to-man pressure style of defense was the same system that was being used throughout the NFL, and a lot of their former players were having good careers there. It was obvious that if you had the talent for the NFL, being at Texas gave you an extra edge.

"The other thing was I became aware of the fact that if you graduated from Texas, you could get a job anywhere in the state, because of the tremendous support system aiding you. UT takes care of its own, and I was impressed with that."

In Gray's case, the first option came through. After a successful career that included a strong run at a national championship in 1983, he signed with the Rams and got enough bonus money to go home and buy his mother a new house.

"When I joined the Rams, they switched me to playing corner, which meant learning a new position," he says. "But because I had just spent four years in a system that prepares you to adapt, the transition was easy."

Establishing himself as one of the best in the league, Gray played on two teams (1985, 1989) that reached the NFC Championship Game and starred in four Pro Bowls. When his career ended, he took some time off to think about the next move.

"Pretty soon," he says, "it dawned on me that I had been involved in football my whole life and had thought quite a bit about getting into coaching."

By that time, he was also a family man.

"Sherry and I had known each other growing up, because our families went to the same church," he said. "But we didn't start dating until I was in L.A. and she was a student at Texas Tech.

"I enjoyed L.A. for a while, and out there, whatever you want is right there for you. But you never really know how real it is.

"I came back to Texas and married someone I knew, a good Christian person who was just interested in Jerry and who has brought so much into my life."

Gray began his coaching career as an assistant at SMU and then got a job with the Oilers. When they became the Titans, he made the move to Tennessee and coached on a Super Bowl team. Then he got the job in Buffalo.

"I really love coaching," he says. "I'd do it for free, but fortunately, they pay me for it."

Except that Gray is more inclined to look upon it as teaching.

"I really do look at it as teaching," he says. "As a teacher, you have to make sure you effect positive change. If I come to work and can't effect change, then I don't figure I did a good job."

Although most of his career has been in the NFL, Gray says he would gladly return to the college ranks for the right opportunity or stay in the pros. Either way, there is a strong focus on teaching young men of a certain age some valuable lessons about life—and money.

"I would love to go back to college [coaching] in the right situation," he says. "The main reason why I got into this job is the chance to affect the minds and futures of guys in the 17-to-22 age range. At that age, you can help set them up for life, and if they get a chance to play pro ball, that's a bonus.

"I see it so often, guys coming in at this level with no idea what to expect, and you can tell there are some things missing there, from high school or college or whatever.

"Things move fast at the NFL level, and it's hard to try to adjust to the style while you're still trying to learn some things about life. I don't mean just technique. I mean things like handling your money and trying to make a family work. You should already know those things before you get here, because they don't have time to teach you your job and that, too."

Although Gray successfully handled the situation himself, he has seen many careers veer off in the wrong direction immediately when young players get caught up in large amounts of money.

"I'm working on putting together a plan where you would actually put on seminars in college for these guys," he says. "If you're lucky enough to win the lottery—which is what I call the big signing bonus—you will be in a position to do a lot of things you've never done, such as, in my case, buy my mother a house. It's a great opportunity if you've been educated about it like I was.

"But if you don't know anything about the IRS, or investments, or [tax] shelters, you can lose it all. A lot of guys, they suddenly have a million dollars, or two million, and they think it's all theirs. If you've never had a friend explain that the IRS will take 36 percent of that, you're in trouble.

"You'd think guys coming out of college would be aware of that, but many of them aren't. I think that it's part of our job as coaches and teachers to correct that."

As for his career ambitions, Gray is aware that—just as there was no premium on minority quarterbacks when he got out of high school 25 years ago—there are still relatively few black head coaches in the NFL or Division I-A college ball.

"Well, there are more in the NFL, because several have now been very successful and blazed a trail that others can follow," he says. "As far as the college situation goes, I heard a guy on the news the other night projecting the idea that the fear of athletic directors is not in hiring minority coaches, but in maybe having to fire them someday. I guess I had never really thought of it that way."

The case of Notre Dame and Tyrone Willingham may be a case in point, but if so, Gray says there's fuzzy thinking afoot.

"As an athletic director, I don't think you should ever be afraid of firing anyone who hasn't done a good job for your program," he says. "Race should not be a factor, and that should not be used as an excuse not to hire a guy.

"Normally, if you hire someone with a strong background and a great track record, he's pretty much going to do the job you want. If you hire someone who doesn't have the track record and you make a mistake, you shouldn't feel bad when you fire that guy.

"If a guy's done a good job over his lifetime and hits a situation that's not working, he should have enough pride to say, 'I'm not doing a good job here, and I don't deserve to get paid for it,' and step down. Why would you stay at a place where you're not doing a good job? It goes to self-pride.

"Athletic directors and [NFL] owners need to understand this: You look at it and say, 'Why are we firing this guy?' If you can justify the decision, you've done enough. If you can't justify it, don't fire him. That should be the same for everyone, not just black coaches.

"It also has to do with the goals of the job. In the NFL, there is one goal for every franchise: Win the title. At some universities they expect to win national championships, and if you take the job, you have to understand that."

Gray has slightly altered his own career timetable but is still basically on track.

"I once set a goal to be a head coach by the time I was 40," he says. "In the last couple of years I interviewed for the Cal job and didn't get it, and turned down an offer to interview for the Syracuse job. Every time I interview for a job, I feel that I learn more about the process and get a little better at it. If the right job comes up or if something opens up in the NFL, I'll be ready.

"I really like what I'm doing."

Where Have You Gone?

A.J. "JAM" JONES

When A.J. Jones came out of Youngstown, Ohio, as a widely recruited *Parade* All-America running back, he was searching for new vistas, a varied life experience, perhaps even a second home.

"Basically, I just wanted to get out of Ohio," he says.

He finally narrowed it down to Southern Cal or Texas. But after he visited Austin, the Trojans were in the rearview mirror.

"When I came down to Texas," he says, "I loved the town, loved the people, felt real comfortable with the players. I just knew this was probably where I needed to be."

For the next four years, things worked fairly close to what Jones had hoped for—he was the team's leading rusher each year and played on four bowl teams, culminating with a victory over Alabama in the 1982 Cotton Bowl.

He finished with 2,874 career rushing yards and only Earl Campbell, Chris Gilbert, and Roosevelt Leaks had ever done better in a Longhorn uniform (he has since been passed by Ricky Williams and Cedric Benson). He scored 27 touchdowns and was drafted by the Los Angeles Rams.

But more than that, in the memory of a wider world, Jones left Texas with something he never figured on—an identity that will follow him throughout his life. When statistics and records have been forgotten, he will be forever remembered as part of the lyrical trio of Ham, Lam, and Jam.

Three guys named Jones—with aliases.

"You know, I think that to this day, those are three of the most recognizable names in college football," says Jones, who has owned or run several businesses in the Los Angeles area since retiring from pro football in the late 1980s. "We're like 45, 46, 47 now, and people still remember who we are."

The funny thing is that Jones—who became Jam—isn't sure exactly where it came from.

A.J. "JAM" JONES
Hgt: 6-2 • Wgt: 195 • Hometown: Youngstown, Ohio

Years played: 1978-1981
Position: Tailback
Highlights: 1978: leading rusher; 1979: leading rusher; 1980: leading
rusher; 1981: leading rusher; ranks sixth on all-time UT rushing list
with 2,874 yards and fifth on list of 100-yard games with 14

"We all played together," he says, "but the other two guys got there a couple of years before me. They were both named Johnny Jones and so to distinguish between them they were nicknamed after their hometowns—Lampasas and Hamlin.

"I was just Anthony Jones from Ohio, and I don't know where 'Jam' came from. I think the coaches just got together and gave me that name. But I'll tell you something—people have never forgotten it.

"I would say it comes up at least once or twice a month. Sometimes it starts because someone hears me say, 'Dang!' and they wonder where I came from. Or maybe it just comes up in conversation that I used to play football.

"And so they ask about it, and I say I played for the Rams and at Texas, and they ask who I am, what's my name? And that's how it comes up.

"And invariably there's this reaction like, 'Get outta here! No way, you gotta be kidding. *You're* Jam Jones? Wow.'"

"Wow" was pretty much the operative description of Jones in the days when, as he recalls, "you would have coaches by the handful showing up at your house every day."

One of these, of course, was Woody Hayes. And he was certainly the most memorable.

"Woody was a different person," Jones says, laughing. "You know, he was a Civil War historian, and when he came to my house, he hardly mentioned football. He just talked to my parents about the Civil War.

"My mom adored Woody. My dad liked him, too, but he and my mom just really hit it off great, and he was a very impressive guy. But I wasn't really thinking that much about Ohio State. For a while I was leaning toward USC, but Texas really impressed me more."

An outright SWC title eluded the Longhorns in Jones's four seasons (1978-1981), but three of those teams were ranked 12th or higher and two finished in the top 10. All four played in bowl games. In Jones's senior year, Texas reached the Cotton Bowl when SWC champion SMU—whose only loss was to Texas—was declared ineligible. The Longhorns rallied in the fourth quarter to beat Alabama and finished the season ranked No. 2 in the nation.

Big games were a feature of Jones's career, and he ranks fifth on Texas's all-time list with 14 games in which he rushed for 100 yards or more. Three of his biggest came in victories over teams ranked in the top 10: Oklahoma in 1979 and 1981 and Arkansas in 1980.

"We played a lot of tough teams every year," he says, "but OU and Arkansas were usually the two biggest games. We beat OU the last three years I was there, and I've got MVP trophies at home from all of them.

"They have a name for those games down there: *slobber knockers*, and that's exactly what they were."

He also remembers a Sun Bowl game as a freshman when he and Ham both rushed for more than 100 yards (Lam was a two-time All-American as a wide receiver).

"Man, we cut up that game," he says. "That's what I'll always carry with me about Texas—the memories and the guys I played with. We were all so close, like family, and those guys still mean the world to me today, although I don't see them as often as I'd like to.

"I met some phenomenal people at Texas—players, students, alumni, it was just a great time. Pro football was fun and a very valuable part of my life, especially since it provided financial security. But it was nothing like college. I love college football."

There is one memory in particular that, Jones says, means a lot to him.

"I can't say enough about Fred Akers," he says. "He's a heckuva man, and I respect him in every way you can respect a person. He was phenomenal. I got to talk to him recently on the phone, and we talked for about an hour.

"I'm so glad I had a chance to talk to him and to thank him for being the kind of person he was to me. He's a class act."

Jones is less pleased with his seven-year NFL career, spent mostly with the Rams and Lions.

"It was okay, but it could have been better," he says. "Actually, I shouldn't complain—I had some nagging injuries, but overall it was fun, and I got out of it with my health and my pension, so all in all it was good. I would also say this: I think that playing at a big school like Texas or Michigan or something like that prepares you pretty well for the NFL. In my case, it really wasn't as big an adjustment as I thought it would be."

But in L.A., Jones became part of a traffic jam that also involved Eric Dickerson and Charles White, and the coach he calls "J.R."

"I just felt that John Robinson never used me the way he said he was going to use me, and I think it hurt my career," he says. "At the time, it was a bummer, and I was really bitter about it. But it's all water under the bridge now.

"It's a business, and that's the way things happen. At the end of my career [in Detroit] I actually sat out a year and then tried to come back, but I just didn't have it. The spirit was still willing, but my legs just weren't there anymore. For a running back, that's a real downer.

"But I had a pretty good career and met a lot of great people, and came out of it pretty good. I was very blessed."

Since then Jones, 46, has built a successful business career in Los Angeles but says the day will probably come when he will move back to Austin.

"I lived in Austin for six years before actually moving out here," he says. "When I left pro ball I just stayed out here, because I had a lot of contacts from playing football, and a lot of business opportunities opened up. I've been here 21 years now.

"This is a fast place, and if you're not prepared for it, it'll swallow you up—I've seen it happen. It's a totally different place. People out here work on making their money; they work on driving nice cars; they work at keeping fit. It's just a certain lifestyle.

"When I left pro ball, I got into the clothing business and eventually went into business with my brother. For a long time we owned three clothing stores up in

Hollywood—Hollywood Boulevard, Melrose—and we catered to a lot of the celebrity trade, and out here there's a lot of it. We did real well, had a lot of celebrity clients, and we did that for about 12 years."

Or until the economy tanked a few years ago. Like many others, Jones and his brother lost their business.

"It completely sucked us dry," he says. "We finally decided to close the stores one by one. It wasn't nice. It wasn't nice at all."

But recovery is in progress in the Jones family.

"One thing I'm doing now is I'm a district manager for a retail service company," he says. "But I've also had my own cleaning business for about four years—I bought a franchise, and it's doing really well.

"This time I'm hoping I've gotten into a really bulletproof business. It seems there are always people who need their business cleaned or their school cleaned or their high-rise cleaned, so I'm doing okay."

He is also going through a divorce.

"It's funny how these things work," he says. "We were together for about seven years, and then about a year and a half ago, we decided to get married. I really thought I was ready to do that, but now it's over. We have a little three-year-old daughter, Jayda."

He also has a grown daughter—Lauren—who is in Austin starting a career.

"She's 22 now," he says. "She grew up in Austin and was an all-star volleyball player at Tulane, and she's getting into sports media. She's interviewed with the Astros and Dallas Mavericks so far."

The Jones brothers, meanwhile, are back in business.

"My brother Michael—he played with the Vikings and in the USFL—he lives in Atlanta now, and he owns a big cleaning franchise. We talk twice a day, and we're doing a lot of real estate together. We just closed on a four-plex in Atlanta, and we've got things going all over the place.

"I also call home every day. My mom and dad have been married for 49 years, and I don't think they make 'em like that anymore. They're enjoying their retirement, and we talk a lot. We're a close-knit family.

"So, you know, L.A. is fun, but I'm older now, and I'd like to stay out here another five years, 10 at the most, and finish up building my retirement.

"But you can count on it. Someday, I'll definitely be heading back to Texas."

Where Have You Gone?

T JONES

When T Jones was growing up on a farm west of Childress during the Depression, it was pretty much understood that just about everything in life came hard.

Certainly, farming was hard, and the six Jones children understood that if they were ever lucky enough to attend college, it would have to be on some kind of scholarship. For the four boys, maybe a football scholarship.

That was also a hard road. When Jones was "about six or seven," an older brother died as the result of a football injury.

"He got hit in the side," Jones said. "That was in the days before penicillin, and he got blood poisoning and died. He was about 15. To add to everyone's grief, right after that, his best friend was also killed playing football when he broke his neck.

"That kind of put a damper on things around Childress for a while, and also made my parents very leery of the idea of the rest of us playing football. For a long time, we just never brought it up."

Eventually, each of the three brothers went to college on football scholarships, although Jones tried his mother's patience by getting kicked in the mouth a couple of times and sacrificing a few teeth.

"That was back in the days before facemasks," he says. "The first time it happened and they brought me home before school was out, my mother was sitting on the front porch. She jumped up, realizing something was wrong. But I got out of the truck and grinned at her—with two front teeth missing—and told her I was okay.

Eventually, Jones became the star quarterback on a championship team at Texas (1952) and then went off for a hitch in the Army.

"I don't know exactly how it came about," he says, "but somewhere in there I realized that what I had always wanted to do was coach. It was what I really loved and wanted to do with my life."

T JONES
Hgt: 6-1 • Wgt: 185 • Hometown: Childress

Years played: 1950-1952
Position: Quarterback
Highlights: 1952: All-SWC

When he got out of the service, Jones was hired at Texas by athletic director Dana X. Bible, and after a coaching change found himself working for Darrell Royal, one of the rising young stars in the profession. By 1963 he was a valued assistant in a program that was about to win a national championship.

Then he quit.

"It was probably the hardest thing I've ever done in my life," he says, "because I was leaving the profession I loved, and I didn't really want to.

"But I had no choice. It was a personal thing, due to the illness my wife had. I didn't know at the time that it was depression. I just knew that she wasn't happy with me coaching. I had two small children and felt I needed to be closer to home instead of traveling around so much.

"So I told Darrell I had to resign. I felt that if I got out of coaching I could make it all okay. But it didn't work, and my wife and I later divorced.

"Anyway, I went to work at the old City National Bank in Austin. A year later, Darrell asked me to come back. I told him, 'There's nothing over this past year I've missed more than coaching. But I've made this decision, and I'd better stick with it.'"

Over the years, Jones has retained vivid memories of what he walked away from.

"Well, first of all, I was lucky that Mr. Bible created the chance for me to get into coaching in the first place," he says. "And when I came out of the service and joined Ed Price's staff in 1956, I was bright-eyed and enthusiastic.

"At that time, I had no idea what I was getting into. The program was in trouble: The staff was split into factions; there was confusion, low morale, disloyalty, and a lot of politics. We went 1-9 and Ed was fired, and there I was one year into the business and out of a job.

"So I was packing up like everyone else when Mr. Bible called and asked me to come to his office. When I got there, Darrell was there, and he introduced us. We talked for a few minutes, and Darrell asked if I could give him a ride to the airport.

"While we were on the way, he asked me if I would stay and be an assistant on his staff. I was thrilled.

"From that point on, it was a totally different situation. Darrell put together a great staff of young coaches, and we started the rebuilding process with great enthusiasm and camaraderie. We were all on the same page, nobody was after the head coach's job, and we began bringing in a lot of talented players.

"At our first staff meeting, the first thing he did was make it clear that there would be no cheating, no illegal recruiting. He said, 'One slip and you're gone; if you don't know the rules, get an NCAA rulebook and read it.'

"As for the rest of it, it was kind of like the [Vince] Lombardi approach: We're working hard to build something here, and if you want to be a part of it, there will be a place for you. If not, you can go over on the sideline and rest a bit."

"I enjoyed those six years. It was fun, being part of turning the program around and creating something good. But I had to go, or thought I did."

T Jones (*Photo courtesy of T Jones*)

Jones remained a banker for 17 years, during which time his kids grew up and he remarried.

In 1980, he got a call from Bill Ellington, who had taken over as athletic director at Texas after Royal retired. With his kids grown and his life stabilized, Jones felt he was ready for a comeback, as assistant athletic director.

But Ellington resigned a year later, and Jones—the presumed heir—suddenly found himself working for DeLoss Dodds.

"At first I thought it might be a kind of awkward situation," he says, "but DeLoss asked me to stay and was very nice to me—still is—and has become a great friend over the years. And he's done a terrific job there."

In 1985, Jones became the athletic director at Texas Tech, hired to revive a sagging program.

"They had kind of hit rock bottom," he says, "short on dollars, facilities in bad shape, worried about NCAA sanctions, recruiting the wrong athletes, and in need of a new academic approach. And they badly needed to upgrade their non-conference schedule."

Jones soon became aware of another pertinent fact.

"I had always known that Tech people didn't like Texas," he says, laughing. "Until then I just never realized that they hated Texas.

"When I got there, I was staying at the Lubbock Inn, and Jess Stiles had arranged to have a car delivered there for me. So the next morning I got in the car to go out to the school.

"The radio was on, and as I'm driving along, this talk show guy comes on and says, 'Well, let me tell Mr. T Jones something—he can just back his moving van up, load all his orange T-shirts in it, and go back to Austin, because he's not welcome in Lubbock.'"

Things got even more interesting when Jones brought in David McWilliams to be the new head coach for the 1986 season.

He turned the program around with a 7-4 year, but in December, Texas fired Fred Akers, and Dodds called McWilliams about coming back to Texas as head coach.

"David came to see me about it, and he was a mess," Jones says. "I said, 'David, you and Cindy have to make that decision. You have a chance to go to one of the most prestigious universities in the country, one with enormous resources, where they can do so much for you as a coach that I could never do. I'm not telling you that I don't want you—I would love to have you stay. But you and Cindy have to make that decision and let me know.'"

McWilliams took the Texas job, and Jones named Tech assistant Spike Dykes as the new head coach.

"Pretty soon," he says, "I got call from a guy who said he 'represented all the alums', and he wanted me to clean out my desk and leave town that day. I said, 'You got anything else on your mind?' and he hung up.

"At that point, I figured the fans were divided into three factions: one-third hated me for the coach I just hired, one-third hated me for the coach that just left, and one-third hated me for being from Texas and taking the job in the first place.

"So I figured if they all hated me, I was at least going to do things my way."

All ended well. Dykes launched a long tenure as a popular successful coach; Jones finally retired in 1993 and has since been enshrined in Tech's Hall of Honor. At the induction ceremony, however, Dykes couldn't resist one last dig.

"When he introduced me," Jones says, "He said, 'The day Tech hired T Jones, all the flags in West Texas flew at half-mast, because everybody knew they'd hired another idiot from Texas.'"

Jones, 74, and his wife, Phyllis, who were married in 1976, now live in retirement at Horseshoe Bay. His son, Mike, does real estate and land development in Austin. His daughter, Manette, a teacher at Westlake High School, died of cancer last year at 48.

"You can always look back over your life and find good and bad," he says. "I guess the decision I made long ago to give up coaching—the thing I loved—still haunts me a little.

"But I'm glad I was raised in Childress, because it was a good place to grow up, and as it turned out, we all did go to college. I remember when I went off to Austin, being amazed at how far away it was."

He left four years later, having quarterbacked a team with an entire All-Conference backfield, with a Cotton Bowl ring and a business degree.

"I'm glad I spent two years in the Army," he says. "I learned some things and grew up a lot. Once they put me in charge of some amphibious landing craft and the commander asked me if I needed any help with anything, I said it would probably help if someone showed me how those things worked, because the biggest thing I had ever been on was a rowboat on a stock tank in Childress, Texas. He really thought that was funny.

"I guess I've traveled a long way since then, and I've been lucky in a lot of ways. These days I still see Darrell and we play golf a lot, and Spike lives down here, and Emory Bellard isn't that far away, and we're in a very pleasant place.

"Can't complain."

Where Have You Gone?

_____

ERNIE KOY JR.

In a life that has now spanned 62 years, Ernie Koy Jr. has circled back around to the place where he started—hanging out at the Five and Dime in Bellville.

To be sure, there were notable side trips along the route, including an outstanding career at the University of Texas in which he played on a national championship team as a junior, and then led the Longhorns to a stunning victory over the nation's top-ranked team in his final game as a senior.

This was followed by six years in the Big Apple as the fullback of the New York Giants, which is also where he met Barbara, a girl from Queens who agreed to become his bride and eventually relocate herself to a small Texas town.

The adjustment went well. They have been married 35 years and have four grown children.

The bright lights were fun for a while, but when Koy left pro football he decided to leave New York City as well. He spent a couple of years as an assistant coach at Sam Houston State and then began drifting toward home.

He has been back for 23 years and although the place has changed some, he still spends a lot of time in one particular spot.

"When we were kids, we were raised in a five-and-ten cent store," says Koy, who is now an officer with the Wells Fargo Bank. "When the store closed years ago, the bank bought the property and eventually some renovations were done.

"So I now have my office in the same place where the store was, in the building I was raised in. I'm back home."

He figures it's a good place to be, especially when life gets a little rough.

When the economy faltered and there were mass closures of banks and savings and loan institutions in the 1980s, Koy believes Bellville survived because of its small-town values and the trust that people placed in each other.

And when Barbara battled breast cancer in 1994, the Koys were again reminded that it's helpful to have a town full of friends.

Koy and younger brother, Ted—who played on the 1969 national championship team and is now a veterinarian in Georgetown—grew up as the sons of a Texas

ERNIE KOY JR.
Hgt: 6-1 • Wgt: 190 • Hometown: Bellville

Years played: 1962-1964
Position: Fullback
Highlights: Rushed for 133 yards in UT's 21-17 upset of top-ranked
Alabama in the 1965 Sugar Bowl

legend. Ernie Koy Sr. (who at 95 still lives in Bellville with his wife, Jane, 93) was a three-time All-Southwest Conference halfback and played several seasons in the major leagues, hitting .279 over a National League career with Brooklyn, St. Louis, Cincinnati, and Philadelphia.

Ernie Jr. launched himself on the road to glory as a storied high school back, who—in a losing cause—starred in one of the most famous games in Texas schoolboy history.

It came in December 1960 in San Angelo, when the Bellville Brahmas and Denver City Mustangs, both unbeaten, collided in a battle for the 2-A state championship.

Bellville was led by Koy and Joe Ed Lynn, Denver City—which scored more than 700 points on the year—by the Gravitt twins, Bert and Bill.

The day before the game, Mustang boosters flashing wads of cash drove through town soliciting bets with anyone they could find from Bellville. They were still at it the next day, standing on the field before the kickoff waving wads of $100 bills at the Bellville fans.

"They were giving some pretty big odds," Koy recalls. "Most of our people had gone out there in a group on a chartered train, and they were kind of a stationary target. As soon as they got off the train, people were waving 50s and 100s at 'em. There was a lot of money bet on that game."

Denver City won 26-21, by withstanding a performance from Koy that included 189 yards rushing, three touchdowns, and a 48-yard punting average.

Mustang fans went home happy—and broke.

"I had a good game, but it wasn't good enough," Koy says. "But the funny thing was that although Denver City won, they didn't cover the spread. So the thing people have always said about it is that Bellville lost the game and won all the money."

After graduation, Koy was heavily recruited but quickly narrowed the choice down to two schools.

"Texas was certainly one of the ones I was thinking about," he says. "At that time Darrell Royal was still building up his program, but when you met him, he was a very impressive individual.

"But LSU was also recruiting me, and I met coach Paul Dietzel and liked him. He was a really nice individual, and they had recently [1958] won a national championship, and Billy Cannon had been a Heisman Trophy winner [1959].

"But then Dietzel announced he was leaving to take the Army job, so that cinched it for Texas."

Well, there was maybe one other wee factor.

"Yeah," Koy says, "my dad did say it would be a lot closer to Austin, and it'd be a lot nicer because Momma could come see me play."

Following in Dad's footsteps, Koy arrived at Texas at a most opportune moment. During his three years on the varsity, the Longhorns went 30-2-1, winning a national championship in 1963 and coming close in 1964.

"Royal really was something special," he says. "Thank God I made the right choice. It was amazing, all the talent that he was bringing in at that time. So many great players—in my class, in the one ahead of us, and in the one behind us."

Although 1963 was a good year for Texas, it was Koy's biggest disappointment as a Longhorn because he missed most of it.

"I got hurt in the Oklahoma State game," he says. "Then I got a staph infection, and I wound up missing the rest of the season."

The following year, Texas was ranked No. 1 and riding a 15-game winning streak when Arkansas came to town in mid-October.

"The games those two teams had back then were really brutal," Koy says. "Neither team passed much, so the fur was really flying down there between the tackles. Third and short meant just exactly that."

Late in the game, with Arkansas leading by a touchdown, Koy led a 70-yard scoring march that left it at 14-13. Disdaining a tie, Royal went for two points and the win.

Royal said later that he thought about running Koy on the two-point play but was afraid he was tired, because he had carried on nearly every play of the touchdown drive. So he opted for a halfback pass, which failed.

Koy rushed for 135 yards, but Texas lost. At the end of the season, Arkansas stood at 10-0 and Texas 9-1. The Longhorns headed for the Orange Bowl to face Joe Namath and top-ranked Alabama.

In his final game for Texas, Koy rushed for 133 yards, and Texas won 21-17, knocking the Crimson Tide out of the No. 1 spot. Ironically, the Texas victory gave the national title to Arkansas.

"I always felt good about my time at Texas," he says. "The one year I missed was a disappointment, but it was a great time to be there."

Pro ball beckoned, but there was a choice to make.

"That was in the days when they had two drafts—the AFL and the NFL," he says. "The AFL held theirs right after the season in late November or early December, and then the NFL had theirs later, in the spring.

"The year before, Scott Appleton was the No. 1 choice in the AFL and went to Houston. In 1965 the Oilers had two top choices and took Lawrence Elkins in one, and then I guess I was the 1A choice.

"I remember that later, Vince Lombardi called and talked to me. But everyone thought that since Appleton and I were friends, I would be joining him in Houston. The Giants had the first choice that year, and they took Tucker Frederickson. They finally drafted me in the 11th round.

"I wound up signing with the Giants."

By way of explaining the decision, Koy offers a brief perspective.

"Well, either way we didn't get a whole lot of money back then like they do today," he says. "I wasn't like, 'Do I go for the $100 million or the $150 million?'

"The AFL was the new league, and I guess being the son of a guy who came up in the Yankee organization when they had Babe Ruth and then playing in Brooklyn, I just wanted to see what it was like up there.

"The Giants had been very good for several years and then had a down year in 1964, so it was kind of the 'here's a chance to come in and help them right away' idea. I had followed the Oilers of course, because they were right there at our back door. Part of it was, 'Do I want to play in Jeppesen Stadium or Yankee Stadium?'

"So I signed for something like $18,000 and a new car. When I got up there, the union was striking for the garbage collectors, and they were all making $12,000 to $15,000. I was the fullback for the Giants and not making a whole lot more."

As far as success on the field was concerned, Koy arrived at just the wrong time to be a Giant.

"Their philosophy had always been to pick up guys—like Y.A. Tittle—who had been good somewhere else, and it had worked well. But when I got there, all the guys they had had gotten old and retired, and the people they brought in didn't have the same impact as before. So it was pretty much the start of a long rebuilding process.

"I played there six years. In 1967 they got Fran Tarkenton, and the next four years were the best I had up there—catching a lot of swing passes out of the backfield. In 1971 he went back to Minnesota, and most of the guys I came in with retired. I really thought I could play another couple of years, but I was married by then, and the Giants suggested I find something else to do."

Koy accepted an offer from his old high school coach, who was at Sam Houston State, and he and Barbara left New York and came to Texas.

"Barbara wanted to teach school and needed to get her teaching certificate, and I wanted to go back and get my master's," Koy says. "So I helped coach the team for two years while we got our other goals done.

"It was a good time for us, and a good way for me to get out of pro football and into something else. I enjoyed the old team spirit and working with the kids, but I didn't enjoy the recruiting and some other aspects.

"At that point I had an opportunity to go with a savings and loan in Brenham, and I took it. It was something I really enjoyed, but I had to work at it, because I was 30 or 31 in a situation where everybody else had started when they were 24.

"I was behind everybody else and I knew it, but I kept going to school and eventually finished the Intermediate Banking School and Graduate School of Banking courses, which are each three years.

"In the meantime, in 1974, I had a chance to go back to Bellville in a savings and loan, so we bought a house and began raising a family, and I think that was a real good decision.

"In 1982 I moved to the Austin County State Bank, which had been here since 1909 and was the bank that bought the store where I grew up and where I now have my office."

Shortly thereafter, the 1980s turned really bad.

"A really bad time," Koy says, "just bad all over. Banks were failing and real estate values were falling, and so many people got caught in the middle. For the first time, the values of land dropped—they had leveled off before, but never dropped. For the first time, the piece of ground you bought was worth less than what you paid for it.

Barbara and Ernie Koy (*Photo courtesy of the Koy family*)

"It was more on paper—the appraisal. The land was still there, but you got a guy paying on a $100,000 house and now it's worth $80,000; it's a shock.

"I remember calling this one old boy about a car loan he was behind on, and finally he just came in one day and pitched the keys on my desk and said, 'Ernie, I know you're worried about this car and I'm worried about it, and there's no sense both of us worrying about it, so you worry about it, 'cause I have to get on with my life.'

"But thank goodness I was sitting here in Bellville, Texas, when it happened. Thank goodness we were lending into a community where there's a character and an attitude about these things that you may not find very often these days.

"So many came in and said, 'Ernie, I can't pay you, but I'm not going to beat you out of it. I'll pay you when I can.'

"And by golly, they did. When we started back with the recovery of 1987, 1988, 1989, we were actually able to expand, because we still had good loans and good people paying on them. We bought some failed banks, including the Sealy National Bank, and we got bigger.

"Eventually, we did all right with that little [Austin Co.] bank. When I came, it was at about $20 million, and when we sold, we were over $110 million. It became Wells Fargo about two years ago. So now I'm the business banker for Wells Fargo for the Sealy and Bellville district."

Meanwhile, Barbara had acclimated herself well to a community that didn't even have a Wal-Mart, never mind a subway system and thrill-seeking cab drivers.

"It was an adjustment," Koy says, "but she finally got used to the idea that everyone in town knows her name and wants to chat. In New York, people are too busy to stop and talk, but with some of these little old ladies here, it's half the day.

"She was a language major, and here she teaches pre-kindergarten and has a lot of Hispanic children who speak Spanish at home, so she catches them at four years old and gets them started with the English language to get them through school. She really enjoys that."

But the enjoyment stopped late in 1994 when Barbara was diagnosed with breast cancer.

"It was unbelievable," Koy says. "She had just had a mammogram in August that indicated she was fine, but by November she told me, 'Something's wrong here.'

"It was finally discovered that although the mammogram was searching for a spot that was growing larger, in her case there were a large number of small spots, and they never formed the pattern they were looking for on the mammogram. It had gone undetected for years.

"It was rough. She had the whole nine yards—surgery, chemo, radiation, the works. But she's tough, and she came through it and bounced back.

"One of the toughest parts was trying to carry on some kind of normal routine with four teenagers in the house. But that's where the small-town character came out again.

"For a year, we never cooked dinner, but there was always food on the plates. People came by and brought food or picked up the kids and took 'em to school or ran errands or—whatever we needed.

"We fought that thing night and day for a year—but we had a whole lot of help. Barbara is back teaching now, and she had a checkup recently and said she's good for another 10,000 miles."

So Koy's life is back to normal—showing up for work at the Five and Dime, checking on his parents, keeping up with his kids.

The oldest, Robert, is currently the offensive backfield coach at Bridgewater College in Virginia. Andy went to the Naval Academy and is an officer on the USS *Russell* at Pearl Harbor. Lucy is the youth director at Saint Mark's Episcopal Church in Houston. Jess is a senior business major at Sam Houston.

"Bellville has changed some, but it's still a small town," Koy says. "We're kinda off the beaten path. Sealy, Brenham, Hempstead, they all have Wal-Marts now. We don't have one, but they're close enough where it's kind of killed all the Mom and Pop's.

"What has survived here is our county was the first settlement, and there's a lot of history here, a lot of old buildings, and we're big into antiques. The first Saturday of each month, there's booths all over town."

As for the way his life has developed, he figures the biggest part of it has been Barbara.

"She got me settled down, headed in another direction," he says. "When you're an athlete, it's all-consuming. It's your total focus at all times. I was that way into my 30s, but it's changed and turned out pretty well.

"If I had it to do over again, I'd pick the same girl."

Where Have You Gone?

BOBBY LACKEY

O ver a period of three or four decades, Bobby Lackey has come to understand that the world of the permanent celebrity can sometimes be confusing.

Oh, it's gratifying that after all these years, people are still sending him copies of that 1958 issue of *Sports Illustrated*, asking him to autograph it.

That would be the one identifying Lackey and young coach Darrell Royal as Texas' knights in shining armor for slaying the fearsome Oklahoma dragon that had terrorized the realm for years.

It's nice that they still remember. It would be even nicer if they could get the names straight.

"Someone sent me one the other day that was a little confusing," he says. "They wanted an autograph from someone named Thomas Clendon, who I had never heard of. Finally, we figured out that they meant Clendon Thomas, who played for OU back then. We finally got it straightened out, but it took a while."

To avoid further confusion:

In 1957 Lackey and Royal became prominent members of the UT program at the same time: Lackey as sophomore quarterback, Royal as designated savior.

As a junior Lackey threw two touchdown passes and then intercepted a pass late in the game to seal the momentous 15-14 victory over the Sooners, who came into the contest ranked No. 2 in the nation, with 52 victories in their last 53 games.

In 1959, Lackey was the starting quarterback on Royal's first Cotton Bowl team at Texas.

This was followed by a brief misadventure with professional football, after which Lackey returned home to Weslaco and spent the next 40 years in the agricultural produce business, the longtime economic mainstay in the Rio Grande Valley.

But, he says, life in The Valley has changed and so has the produce industry, and the free trade agreement has not necessarily been good for all North Americans. He watched an 80-year-old company die and then retired four years ago. There was a double bypass in 2000, but he figures he "got through that okay."

BOBBY LACKEY
Hgt: 6-0 • Wgt: 180 • Hometown: Weslaco

Years played: 1957-1959
Positions: Quarterback, defensive back
Highlights: Led 1959 team to a No. 4 national ranking, the first SWC
championship and Cotton Bowl team of Darrell Royal era

About a year ago he and his wife, Judy—who have been married for 48 years—moved to Spring to be near their daughters, Melissa and Mindy. A son, John, is a financial planning specialist in Weslaco.

They remember Lackey well down there, where through the years he served on the school board, the city commission, and the board of a local bank. He did a stint a president of the chamber of commerce and—for five years—president of the hospital board.

At the high school, where he once played and later created a scholarship, the gymnasium and football field are both named after him.

Meanwhile, up in the Houston area, life ain't bad. Lackey spends time with old Southwest Conference acquaintances King Hill (Rice) and Vernon Hallbeck (TCU), runs into old Longhorns Bob Moses and the Talbert brothers, maintains his long-time connection with Royal, and limits himself to golfing "only on days that end in y."

And every once in a while, another old copy of *Sports Illustrated* lands in the mailbox, and the reel of the mind spins backward in time....

In 1955 Lackey led Weslaco to the 2-A state semifinals and became a member of a highly prized group of senior quarterbacks that caught every eye in the Southwest Conference.

"I was highly recruited—we all were," he says. "It was me, Don Meredith from Mount Vernon, Larry Dueitt from Corpus Christi, Charles Milstead from Tyler, and the kid from New London, Jackie Sledge.

"People were saying it was the most sought-after group of quarterbacks in the history of the state, and every time a recruiter would come around, they would put all of us on a list and they'd point at it and say, 'See? We've got you at the top of the list.' Of course, when they went down the road to talk to the next guy, he was on the top of the list.

"All five of us played in the all-star game in Lubbock—me, Dueitt, and Milstead for Bear Bryant's team and Meredith and Sledge for Abe Martin's team."

Each coach got something out of it: Milstead went with Bryant to A&M, while Sledge chose TCU. Dueitt wound up at Rice and Meredith at SMU.

"I was actually the first one to commit," Lackey says, "and then they all went pretty quick after that. It's funny—at the time, Texas was one of my last choices. Rice, SMU, and TCU were after me pretty strong, and I was actually kind of leaning toward Baylor, because I was a Baptist and I guess I thought that's what I ought to do. Then there was a Methodist preacher down in McAllen pushing me to go to SMU.

"But I had a friend who was a referee, and he took me to the state basketball tournament over in Austin, and later he took me to the state [SWC] track meet, where I saw Bobby Morrow run against Eddie Southern.

"I really enjoyed that, and I thought, 'Hey, this is the greatest place in the world to go to school, because I can go see all these state meets every year.' So that's how I chose Texas."

As a freshman in 1956, he watched the program go down in the flames of a 1-9 season in the final year of the Ed Price regime.

"There was a lot of bickering going on among the coaches, and the staff was split into different groups, and there wasn't much cooperation," he says. "It was horrible, but it was not something that was apparent during the recruiting process.

"Then they brought Royal in, and from the first time he walked into the room at a team meeting, you could tell things had changed. He was pretty blunt and plain-spoken, and he had a certain swagger to him that let you know he was definitely in charge."

And, Lackey figured, he was in trouble.

"Ironically," he says, "another reason why I chose Texas was because they were throwing the ball quite a bit back then, and that's what I wanted to do. In fact, other schools would use that as a recruiting thing. They would point out that Texas already had Walter Fondren, Joe Clements, and Vince Matthews, and they told me I'd have no chance to play.

"But Darrell put a stop to all that. We didn't work on passing much.

"In fact, that first spring I was running at like first or second string in the drills, and that's the only reason I stayed. I thought seriously about transferring to Hardin-Simmons, because Sammy Baugh was the coach out there, and they were throwing the ball."

Fortunately, Lackey stayed and played on Royal's first team—which produced an amazing turnaround with a 6-3-1 record and a trip to the Sugar Bowl. It was a forgettable experience—a 39-7 loss to Ole Miss—but it was a tad better than 1-9. By that time, Lackey had also married Judy McManus.

"We had known each other in high school, but we didn't date then," he says. "She was a cheerleader and was actually a year ahead of me. We started dating the summer of 1956 after I got out of high school and got married the next year."

As for the Longhorns, the 1957 turnaround had been nice, but they were looking for something bigger in 1958—and they got it when Oklahoma arrived for the annual battle in the Cotton Bowl.

The Sooners, coached by Royal's old mentor, Bud Wilkinson, had beaten Texas six straight times—usually by substantial margins—and had won nine of the last 10 games in the series.

It was the most searing wound to Longhorn pride that anyone could have imagined, and it had begun to seem as if it would go on forever. But in 1958, for the first time in years, both teams came into the game undefeated.

"The biggest thing I remember," Lackey says, "is that 1958 was the first year of the two-point conversion in college football, and before the game Coach Royal told Don Allen, our fullback, 'If we score first, we're going for two—and we'll give you the ball, and you'll be one on one against Prentice Gautt to get into the end zone, so be ready.'

"Well, we scored first—I threw a touchdown pass to Rene Ramirez—and we ran that play and Allen got into the end zone for two points and we led 8-0. Those were the only two points Allen scored in his career at Texas, but they were huge."

The Sooners came back to eventually take a 14-8 lead, but with Matthews at quarterback in the fourth quarter, the Longhorns drove down to the OU seven-yard line, where Royal sent Lackey back in to execute a specific play.

"It was a jump pass to Bob Bryant, and it worked for the touchdown," says Lackey, who then kicked the game-winning extra point and later intercepted a pass to shut down OU's final threat. "So we won 15-14 on the margin of the two-point conversion.

"Looking back, I think that was a huge game—maybe the biggest win Texas had had up to that time and certainly one of the biggest ever. It was the turnaround for Darrell and his program. It was a big help to recruiting, and it kind of sent him off to the races.

"It changed a lot of attitudes and got a big monkey off our back. With that win, he beat Oklahoma eight straight times and 12 out of 13."

Later in the season the Longhorns ran afoul of TCU, SMU, and Rice—the block bullies of the day—and finished 7-3. But a big corner had been turned.

In 1959 the Longhorns won their first eight games and were ranked No. 2 when they were beaten 14-9 by TCU. But they recovered to beat the Aggies, finish 9-1, and wind up in a three-way tie with Arkansas and TCU for the SWC championship (all three teams were ranked in the top 10). With a No. 4 national ranking, Texas drew the Cotton Bowl assignment against unbeaten Syracuse, the No. 1 team in the nation.

"They were a terrific team," Lackey says. "Big, fast, great defense, good quarterback, super running back [Ernie Davis]. They deserved to be No. 1, but we played a great game against them. We put up a fight."

In his final game, Lackey accounted for both Texas touchdowns—throwing a 69-yard touchdown pass to Jack Collins and later scoring on a one-yard run—as the Longhorns lost 23-14. He finished his career as one of the cornerstones on the Texas program's rise from mediocrity to national prominence.

"After that I signed with Pittsburgh," he says, "but I only stayed about a week and then jumped the club. There was a guy, a linebacker, who went with me. I dropped him off in Cleveland and then drove home. I drove nonstop to Austin, stopped and slept for a couple of hours, and then drove back to Weslaco.

"When I got home, the Steelers called and we talked, and they talked me into coming back. So I went to Brownsville, caught one of those old prop jobs, and flew back to California, Pennsylvania, where there camp was. Art Rooney Jr. met me at the airport.

"So I tried it again, but it just didn't work. Buddy Parker was the coach, and Bobby Layne was the quarterback, and I think one reason why they were so anxious for me to stay was they needed someone in case he got hurt.

"The thing was, I loved the football part. We were throwing the ball, and that's what I wanted to do. It was the rest of it that was bad. What we mostly had on that team were not exactly the best type characters you would want to be around. I liked the football, but the surroundings were really bad. I've been told that these were not the best type people in the game, and that was the way I felt.

"It wasn't really big money. My contract was for $11,000, with a $1,500 bonus. But Layne was only making about $20,000, and Ernie Stautner, who was an All-Pro, was making $7,500. Parker wanted me to stay until we played an exhibition game in New Orleans—he said I'd be closer to home then if I still wanted to jump—but I said no and left.

"This time when I got home, I got a call from the Boston Patriots in the new league [AFL], but Pittsburgh owned the rights to me, so I called Parker to see if he would release me. He said to have [Boston] call him. That's the last I ever heard from either of them.

"So I came home and went to work for my father-in-law, who owned the McManus Produce Company, and I've never had a regret about pro football. It might have been different if I'd gone somewhere else, but I never worried about it."

He went to work farming and packing fruits and vegetables and watched his kids grow up. Both girls played college basketball—Melissa at Schreiner in Kerrville when it was still a junior college, Mindy for four years at Southwestern in Georgetown. John also went to Schreiner and played golf, and then finished up in San Marcos at Southwest Texas State.

"He was in the produce business with me, but now he's in securities, insurance, and family planning. Mindy's here in Spring in the same business John's in. In fact, he got her started in it. When Schreiner went four years, Melissa was the first person they offered a scholarship to, but she decided to come home. She's got a vending machine business now here in Spring."

As for the ag business, Lackey says, it was good while it lasted.

"McManus is not in operation anymore," he says. "It was an 80-year-old company when it folded. The ag business in South Texas just got kind of sour.

"We were doing a lot of vegetables. Fruits, we weren't doing the oranges and grapefruits, just cantaloupes and honeydews. Things got bad when the free trade hit us—with that, everything came across the border from Mexico and the Caribbean without any duty on it, and with their labor costs down there, it really hurt South Texas agriculture.

"There are not that many people left in it now, really. Some are still doing well, but the produce business has changed. Wal-Mart has become a big player by getting people to sell at a price—knowing what [price] you're going to get is something you didn't have back in the old days when it was a roll of the dice every day. Now they do contracts with Mexican farmers where it's pre-sold at a set price.

"We used to have 200 shippers, but they aren't growing much in The Valley these days, except for co-ops. There are very few independent farmers, and I don't think even the Hunts [Lamar Hunt] are doing much now. If you're packaging this stuff now, you just about have to grow it yourself or pay to have it grown.

"A lot of it is just competition from Mexico. Our costs escalated tenfold, but our product remained the same. We were getting the same price for produce when I got out that we were getting 30 years ago. The same $10 a ton, but you can't live on it now. Production in South Texas never increased, because the weather is so unpredictable. Down here, only fools and newcomers try to predict the weather.

"So some years you can make it, and others you go bust. If you're growing peppers, your crop can disappear, because little mites that the entomologists can't even find come up from Mexico and eat your crop. They don't realize that the Rio Grande is an international border. They just come up here and eat your crop.

"Really, I'm glad I'm out of it now. I guess my biggest regret is that we didn't have more control over our own destiny.

"So I just decided to come up here and be with my daughters and play golf with my friends."

ROOSEVELT LEAKS

Throughout a life that has had its share of peaks and valleys, Roosevelt Leaks has usually managed to exude a remarkable air of permanence. Once his gaze becomes fixed on something, it tends to stay there.

Signing a contract after departing the University of Texas, he embarked on a nine-year career in pro football—well beyond the norm for an NFL running back.

He has maintained a residence in Austin since he was a student at UT.

He and Beverly, his wife, met 30 years ago on a blind date that became permanent.

Long before he quit the NFL, he became involved in the real estate business and has stuck with it ever since. He is currently a director of appraisals for the veterans land board.

He still makes trips back to the farm in Brenham where he grew up and where he still runs cattle. His parents, Roosevelt Sr. and Eugenia, have lived there for more than 50 years.

And three decades after a decision that probably cost him a lot of money and maybe a Heisman Trophy, he says he wouldn't change it.

He laughs wryly at the thought but says, "When I make decisions, I go ahead with them, right or wrong. If they're wrong, I just have to live with it, but I'm not going to change anything. If I had to make that decision today, I'd probably do the same thing."

The decision came in the fall of his senior year at UT. In his first two seasons, Leaks had become an All-American and rushed for more than 2,500 yards. He had had 12 games with more than 100 yards. In a 1973 game against SMU, he rushed for 342 yards, breaking a 23-year-old SWC record. It would remain the all-time UT standard until Ricky Williams had a 350-yard game in 1998.

Going into the 1974 season, he was generally considered the leading candidate for the Heisman Trophy, having finished third in the voting the previous year. Then, in spring drills, he suffered a knee injury.

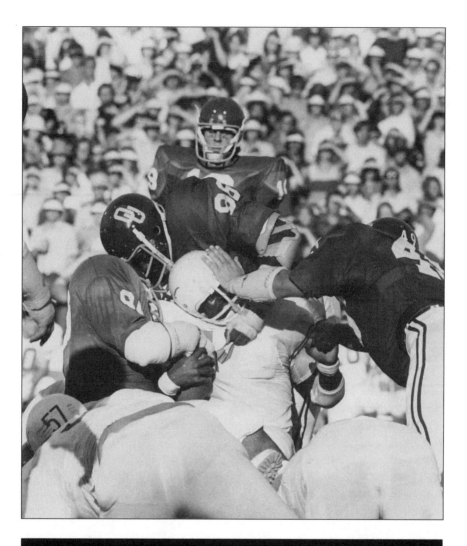

ROOSEVELT LEAKS
Hgt: 5-11 • Wgt: 215 • Hometown: Brenham

Years played: 1972-1974
Position: Fullback
Highlights: 1972: All-SWC; 1973: All-SWC, Consensus All-American;
finished third in Heisman Trophy voting; rushed for 342 yards against
SMU in 1973, second-highest single game total in UT history; ranks fifth
on all-time UT rushing list with 2,923 yards and sixth with
12 games of 100 yards or more

"Just a freak accident," he says. "I went up in the air, and a guy hit me with his helmet. Basically, it just tore the knee apart. With the surgery I had, about 95 percent of guys would probably never play again.

"They told me it would be six to eight months before I could try to play on it. As it happened, six months fell on the day two-a-days started. Coach [Darrell] Royal told me it was my decision whether I wanted to play or take a red-shirt year. And I said, 'I'm playing.'

"I played, but I was never full strength and had a bad year."

The torch passed to a freshman named Earl Campbell. When the NFL draft came in the spring, Leaks was not forgotten, but he felt somewhat reduced.

"Baltimore took me in the fifth round, and you don't even want to know what I signed for," he says. "The difference between that and being a first-round pick was probably way up in six figures, maybe even seven figures. But that's life."

At that, Leaks had already traveled a long road from the days on the farm in Brenham.

"That's what I was raised with," he says. "I lived on a farm, mainly worked in the fields. We raised cotton, corn, and just about anything else. It was country living back in the 1950s and 1960s. My dad was a farmer and day laborer.

"It was hard living, hard work. But we made it through and prospered, although you'd wonder about it from one time to the next.

"We also played ball a lot—baseball, mostly. We didn't have leagues or anything, but we'd just play town against town.

"I had no idea back then about going to college. Very few of us from my area ever went to school—you just got out of high school, got a job, got married, and starting having kids.

"Fortunately, in my case, athletics played a big part in it."

Widely recruited, Leaks was set on going to Houston until he realized that the Cougars' recruiting class included three other running backs. So he signed with Texas, his second choice. That same year, Julius Whittier became the first black football player to letter at UT.

"I guess a lot of people have always had the perception that I was the first black player at UT, because I got a lot of publicity, and Julius didn't because he played in the line," Leaks says. "But that isn't what was on my mind at the time. My main concern was just getting to play.

"There was some friction before my sophomore year about whether I would be the starter if I came out of spring drills at No. 1. It was decided I would be, and it was resolved.

"I knew I would be looked at closely because I was black, and it was not an easy chore. But it was nothing unusual. It was no different from the way it had been in high school. We had been dealing with it all of our lives, and we knew how to handle ourselves."

Leaks also handled himself in the NFL, playing five years with Baltimore and four with Buffalo. Oddly, re-injuring the knee may have helped his longevity.

Roosevelt Leaks (*Photo courtesy of the Leaks family*)

"In my third year," he says, "a big lineman fell on me and bent me backward. My knee went one way, and the rest of me went the opposite direction. It seemed really bad.

"But when the doctors examined me, they found that it had just stretched all the ligaments, and all I needed was rest and rehab—no more surgery. So between that year and the next one, I played eight games, and my body had time to recover.

"If I had played all my career the way I played those first three years, my body would have been beaten up pretty bad.

"When I went to camp for my 10th year, there were five of us [running backs] left out of 150 that had come in a decade before. By the end of that year there was only one—Walter Payton.

"I knew what was coming. When we broke camp, they said, 'Are you going to rent a place?' And I said, 'Nah, I think I'll just stay in a hotel for a week and see what happens.' They cut me, but I understand that. It's a business."

By that time, both Leaks and his wife had been selling real estate for years. In the 1980s, that was also a job that could be injurious to one's health, at least financially.

"I've been through my ups and downs," Leaks says. "I've got my battle scars. I got into real estate in partnership with a couple of doctors and a couple of other athletes more than 25 years ago. I went out on my own for a while, then got into my current job about 15 years ago.

"I work with a staff of 23 appraisers scattered across the state, and we have conversations every Monday morning. We appraise houses and raw land and do foreclosures all across the state. Basically, the property is earmarked for veterans' home sites, or for recreational purposes or hunting."

Leaks says he enjoys the job and feels that it serves a useful purpose.

"It's for the benefit of veterans, and our interest rates are probably lower than any on the market," he says. "Basically, what we ask of a vet buying a home is five percent down, where 10 or 20 percent is probably more typical of the market. We also finance it for 30 years. They can keep it in the family or trade it in, as they choose.

"It's a completely self-supporting business—very self-sufficient. We do sell bonds, some tax-exempt, but there's no need to go into the taxpayer's pocket."

At 52, Leaks figures on doing this long enough to get his kids through school. Printiss, 21, is at Alabama State on a track scholarship, while Sabrina, 14, is a student in the Manor school system.

"Once I get the kids through school, I can retire and go back to the homeplace and tend my cows," he says. "We're still on the same land, but the old farm is mostly hay meadow now. I just make sure everything is paid for and current. My folks bought that place the year before I was born, and someday I'm going back.

"Looking back on my time at Texas, I have no problem with it. I got a degree [communications] and a chance to play pro ball. When I talk to kids today, I stress the education part.

"Athletics they can take away from you. Education is forever."

But some things athletic are not so soon forgotten. Recently Leaks was announced as one of 2005's inductees into the College Football Hall of Fame.

Where Have You Gone?

ALAN LOWRY

Though rare, it occasionally happens that a college football player departs his alma mater leaving behind a particular legacy: a specific moment so brilliant—or controversial—that it is never forgotten.

Such is the fate of Alan Lowry.

Throughout his life, for more than 30 years, wherever he has gone, the former Texas quarterback has been followed by the question: Did you or didn't you?

It refers to one of the final moments of his career—an electrifying 34-yard sprint for the winning touchdown in a 17-13 victory over Alabama in the 1973 Cotton Bowl game.

Capping an 80-yard drive late in the fourth quarter, the run lifted the spirits of Longhorn fans everywhere. It also created an enduring controversy because some claimed that Lowry's left foot had kicked the sideline chalk at the 10-yard line, meaning he ran out of bounds, though the officials didn't call it.

And so, Alan—

"Yeah, I did step on the line," he says. "In fact, I've got a photograph at home that shows it very clearly. But it was over 30 years ago, and the score is still 17-13."

Fortunately, that fact was emphatically stressed moments after the game by the losing coach, Bear Bryant.

"Aw, it don't matter," he said. "They would have eventually scored anyway."

Thus, the situation never developed into a bitter "We Wuz Robbed" controversy. It is just a topic of spirited conversation that has followed Lowry throughout a lengthy coaching career and has been a regular feature in annual Cotton Bowl previews.

"The first thing that comes to mind about that day is that I was sick as a dog," he says. "I'd had 103- to 104-degree temperature, and nothing was open on New Year's Eve, so they couldn't find me any medicine.

"They finally got me something late that night, but it didn't really kick in until halftime the next day. I had a lousy first half, but I felt much better in the second half, and we started playing well.

ALAN LOWRY

Hgt: 5-10 • Wgt: 186 • Hometown: Irving

Years played: 1970-1972
Positions: Quarterback, defensive back
Highlights: 1971: All-SWC as defensive back; 1972: All-SWC
quarterback; scored winning touchdown against Alabama in the 1972
Cotton Bowl

"As for stepping on the line on the touchdown run, it happened when I stepped to plant my foot and cut back inside the defensive back. On the photo, you can see my foot touching the line.

"But at the time, I was completely unaware of it, and nobody said anything about it. [Alabama] didn't say anything, the officials didn't do anything, and in a few minutes the game ended.

"The first time I heard about it was when some reporters came into the locker room talking about it. And I was like, 'Really?'"

Over the years, the incident has almost taken on the aspect of an old pal.

"Actually, it's been a great experience," says Lowry, currently the special teams coach with the Tennessee Titans. "I still run into people wanting to do the joke about the ref saying, 'He was in by this much,' and giving the Hook 'em sign.

"It's been fun to have that memory and [to be] a part of the activities every year when the Cotton Bowl is played. It's fun to be a part of history."

Lowry probably never figured on such a singular claim to fame coming out of Irving High School as a highly sought recruit in 1969. At that point, he wasn't even figuring on a coaching career.

His major focus, in fact, was on something that would soon disappear from his life completely.

"Originally," he says, "I planned on being a radio-TV-film major, thinking I might become a sports broadcaster, that type of thing. But as it turned out, all the classes for that major were held in the afternoon, when I had football practice.

"So since I had a brother who was a coach, I figured maybe that's what I was destined for."

He also became one of the early Wishbone quarterbacks, leading Texas to a 10-1 record and a No. 3 national ranking as a senior.

"I stayed on for a fifth year finishing my degree and served as a graduate assistant," he says. "I think I picked up a lot that year, from both Darrell Royal and Fred Akers."

The next year, his first full-time job was as an assistant at Virginia Tech, and in 1975 he was hired by Akers, who had become the head coach at Wyoming.

"The next year, I came home," he says. "My mother had become very ill with leukemia, so I came back to Irving. I worked with Gil Brandt, grading film in the Dallas Cowboys scouting department.

"My dad died when I was in college, and my mom died that year I came back to Irving. I guess the toughest thing in my life was losing both parents by the time I was 26. But at least I got to be with my mom the last six weeks, there in the hospital."

He also became well acquainted with Donna, his mother's nurse. They have been married for 26 years and have two daughters, Marta and Lindsay.

When Akers succeeded Royal as the Longhorns' head coach, he hired Lowry, who remained as a Texas assistant for five seasons (1977-1981), before moving on to a nine-year stint with the Cowboys, seven under Tom Landry and two under Jimmy Johnson.

He then spent a year in Tampa Bay and four with San Francisco, during which he coached on a Super Bowl championship team. In 1996, he joined the Houston Oilers, who moved to Tennessee and became the Titans the following year.

"So I've been with this organization for nine years now, been to another Super Bowl, enjoying life," he says.

Although he has never been a head coach, Lowry—who has coached offense, defense, and special teams as an assistant—figures he spent a large chunk of his life with the top of the line organizations at two levels.

"It was a thrill for me to be able to come back and coach at Texas," he says. "And it was another thrill to be with Dallas. I went to the first game the Cowboys ever played in 1960. Back then you could get six kids in for one adult ticket, and my dad would take 12 kids to the games.

"I would say there's no question, if you've coached at Texas and Dallas, you've been with the best in college and pro."

Having also spent time around two legends—Royal and Landry—he feels the two were remarkably similar.

"Coach Royal was a very well-organized guy and knew how to handle players really well," he says. "Wasn't a real rah, rah guy. He stayed pretty even keel and concentrated on trying to outcoach you.

"Landry was the same way. Both were very innovative, both stressed the kicking game before that was a general priority. They both came up with different offensive and defensive schemes and formations just to throw the other team off.

"One thing about Landry: I don't think anyone in pro ball will ever again do what he did—put in both the offensive and defensive game plans every week and then call all the plays on Sunday."

Lowry has distinct memories of the sequence in which Landry, after 29 years as the only coach in franchise history, lost his job.

"We were in meetings planning our offseason schedule," he says. "He had just hired a new offensive coordinator and a new defensive coordinator, and we were doing our planning sessions.

"Someone would come to the door, and he would have to leave for a while. He kept having to leave the meetings and was in and out the whole time. Two days later, he wasn't the coach anymore.

"A shock? Yeah—you could say that."

At 54, Lowry feels he has a near-perfect life and has no particular desire for a head-coaching job.

"I think everyone wants that when they first get into coaching," he says. "I've had some interviews through the years, and it didn't happen, and it doesn't bother me. I think that now, I don't really have that aspiration.

"I have a great job and a great family, and a chance to take family vacations and spend time outdoors, which I love to do. In the summers we go to Colorado and hike, but Tennessee is also a great place for outdoor activities. Nashville is great, and so are the fans.

"I have no complaints."

Where Have You Gone?

BUD McFADIN

Wartime shortages being what they are, Bud McFadin probably should have figured he would have to pull duty anywhere the whims of fate demanded. Still, this one was a little weird.

McFadin had completed the 1950 season at Texas as a consensus All-American, the defensive player of the year in the Southwest Conference, and the Longhorns' Most Valuable Player in the 1951 Cotton Bowl.

Then he was picked in the first round of the NFL draft by the Los Angeles Rams. But there was a war going on, and McFadin—like most other athletes coming out of college in that era—had a stretch in the service to do first.

"Under a prearranged deal, I went straight into the Air Force for 18 months after I got out of school," he says. "It was either that or be drafted into the Army."

But in late fall of 1952, with the Korean War stalemated in peace talks and pressing concerns developing elsewhere, an odd thing occurred.

"The Rams came and got me," he says. "I was still in the service at Carswell Air Force Base in Fort Worth, and the Rams made a deal to get me an early release. They had three games left in the season, and they'd had a lot of injuries, and they said they needed me.

"I told them I really didn't think it made much sense, since I didn't know any of their plays. They said they would pay me $3,500 for three games."

The modern NFL operative would not play three minutes for $3,500, but half a century ago, it was a small fortune. McFadin was soon on a plane for L.A.

Besides, he had already spent most of that lavish signing bonus, eh, Bud?

McFadin laughs. And laughs. And continues laughing.

"What bonus?" he says. "The only thing I got for being a first-round pick was a contract for $9,000 a year. Of course, that was a lot of money back then. Norm Van Brocklin, one of the team's biggest stars, was only getting $20,000, so I felt pretty good."

BUD McFADIN
Hgt: 6-3 • Wgt: 240 • Hometown: Iraan

Years played: 1948-1950
Positions: Offensive guard, defensive guard
Highlights: 1949: All-SWC, All-American; 1950: All-SWC,
Consensus All-American

For McFadin, who had grown up on a ranch near the small West Texas town of Iraan (pop. 850), it was the beginning of an association with professional football that lasted 20 years. When it was over, he basically returned to his roots.

"The last job I had was as a coach with the Oilers, which was also the last team I played for," he says. "At that time, I was running some cattle on a place up near Houston.

"Then about 30 years ago, my wife and I moved down here where we are now, in Mission Valley, which is about eight miles south of Victoria. I ranched for a long time, but over all those years it got to be a constant struggle. So now, at 76, I'm working again.

"I work for a company called Air Equipment Rental, based in Victoria and Alice. I travel around to all these oil rigs and talk to the consultants drilling the wells, giving them our price on running the pipe and on equipment, trucks, tools, and a lot of other stuff.

"I still have some horses and some heifers scattered around, just to remind me of where I came from. But I don't have any kin left in West Texas, so I don't get out there much anymore."

Recalling where he came from, McFadin says, "My daddy took care of 25 sections for an old man out there before eventually getting his own place over toward Sanderson, so ranching was what we did, and it was all we knew.

"I never could figure out how all those college recruiters found me out in the middle of nowhere, but they did. Texas sent [assistant] Buddy Jungmichel out there, and he lived with us for about two weeks. By the time I signed, he was no stranger to the family."

Playing offensive guard and defensive tackle, McFadin was a two-time All-American at Texas and had grown to six foot three and 240 pounds by his senior year, primed for pro ball.

But his first post-Longhorn experience wasn't with the Rams. It was with the Carswell Bombers.

"I was stationed at Carswell the whole time I was in the service, playing football," he says. "The coach was Bobby Dobbs, the old Tulsa quarterback. We had a whole lot of college stars, and we won every game we played.

"Once we went out and played a team in San Angelo and beat 'em something like 89-0. I was actually kind of hoping we'd hit 100, so I could say that once I played in a game we won 100-0. But we played every sub we had and never quite made it."

When McFadin made it to the NFL, he encountered a world full of memorable characters.

"When I first arrived at their camp," he says, "they were all inside watching a game film. I opened the door, still carrying my luggage, and it was dark in there, and they all turned to look at the door, and I thought, 'God, these guys look older than my daddy.'"

The two biggest stars were the quarterbacks, Van Brocklin and Bob Waterfield.

Van Brocklin was known for his volatile temper and, McFadin says, "When things weren't going right, it was a good idea to stay away from him."

Waterfield, in addition to his on-field skills, was famous as the husband of film star Jane Russell, whom McFadin got to know quite well.

"I always thought she was a real sweet gal," he says. "Bob always said she was meaner'n hell."

The jury may be out on that one, but meaner than hell is definitely the *Webster's* definition of San Francisco linebacker Hardy Brown, who came out of Fort Worth's Masonic Home High School to carve a reputation in the NFL for knocking people cold with his famed forearm shiver.

"In those days, we didn't wear facemasks," McFadin says. "Sometimes he would have that forearm curled in tight and tied down with a leather harness, like a club, and he could really zap you. There's a lot of people who could tell you about that if you could find them alive."

McFadin played in one NFL title game with the Rams and was twice named All-Pro. But by 1960 he was out of the game and thought his career was over.

Then along came the AFL. McFadin was signed by Denver, where he made All-Pro three more years (1962-1964), making him one of the first to achieve that status in both leagues.

He then played two years with Houston and closed out his career with five years as an assistant with the Oilers. In 1973 he was inducted into the National Football Foundation Hall of Fame.

He has two daughters from his first marriage: Barbara, who has five daughters and lives in Kerrville, and Paige, who lives in Colorado and is the mother of recent Longhorn star Tillman Holloway.

He and his second wife, Patsy, have a son working with the Victoria Electrical Service Plan and another who is a priest in El Paso.

"I guess I could say I've had a fairly interesting life," he says. "So far, I've enjoyed it."

Where Have You Gone?

BOB McKAY

W hen Bob McKay was a schoolboy star playing Class 2-A football in a small West Texas town, he assumed that the people running the college programs in the big cities to the east probably didn't even know where Crane was.

The assumption was based on pure logic—something that has pretty much been McKay's faithful companion throughout a successful life. Fortunately, in this case it was faulty.

So McKay was a bit stunned when he was called to the coaches' office one day to meet Texas assistant coach Mike Campbell, who had come to see if he was interested in becoming a Longhorn.

It didn't take much effort on Campbell's part. When McKay visited Texas and was offered a scholarship by Darrell Royal, he took it.

"I was just glad they found me," he says.

So were the Longhorns. Known as "Big Un"—he was six foot six, 245 pounds as a senior—McKay blossomed into an All-American playing on a national championship team in 1969, then became a first-round draft pick who spent nearly a decade in the National Football League.

Also, McKay has always seemed to draw on some sort of West Texas logic when making decisions about his life, his future, or just how he feels about things: look life square in the eye, make a blunt assessment, try not to overcomplicate things. It works for McKay, although it has sometimes distressed others.

There was, for instance, the recruiting pitch about how a kid from a small town could get himself lost in a big university.

"They'd tell me that at Texas, there would be so many players coming in that I would get swallowed up, lost in the shuffle. I'd get culled and never play at all. But if I came to their school, I'd be able to play right away.

"So I would always say, 'Well, if I'm not good enough to play at Texas, what makes you think you can beat Texas with me playing for you?'"

That one usually crossed a few eyes.

BOB McKAY
Hgt: 6-6 • Wgt: 245 • Hometown: Crane

Years played: 1968-1969
Position: Offensive tackle
Highlights: 1969: All-SWC, Consensus All-American

When Texas Tech coach J.T. King said he couldn't understand why a good ol' boy from West Texas would want to go way off to Austin to school, McKay said, "Coach, I've already been to Lubbock."

He can still muster up a tone of disgust when he recalls sitting in front of the TV, watching "that debacle in 1966, when Notre Dame and Michigan State played to a 10-10 tie in that national championship showdown. When Notre Dame had the ball at the end, I couldn't believe they just sat on it and took the tie. If you're going to play that way, what the hell do you need a scoreboard for?"

He would soon play in a game like that himself, but fortunately, for a coach who famously looked at it the same way he did.

And years later, when his NFL career was through and he was back in Austin trying to figure out the next move, a simple solution presented itself.

"One day I walked into a store to buy some tires, and someone offered me a job," he says. "I've been in the tire business for the last 23 years."

The son of Charles and Doris McKay, he grew up amid the West Texas oil fields.

"My dad worked for Atlantic Richfield—ARCO, and my mom worked for the sheriff's department," he says. "Basically she worked in the office, but she was also deputized to handle female prisoners."

By the end of his senior season in high school, all of those recruiters who McKay figured were ignorant of Crane's geographical location had somehow showed up at the high school looking for the big lineman.

"I followed Southwest Conference football all my life," he says. "I grew up listening to Kern Tips's broadcasts, and to me, that was college football. I remember watching the Cotton Bowl on TV when Texas played Navy. Back in those days, guys like Johnny Treadwell, Duke Carlisle, Pat Culpepper, David McWilliams—they were heroes.

"So I was pretty attuned to going to Texas, and after they offered the scholarship, the rest of the recruiting stuff didn't matter, and I really wasn't interested in taking trips. I had relatives who lived in Los Angeles, and I'd visited them, so I wasn't as ignorant of the outside world as it might seem."

He did take one trip, though, that was kind of fun.

"I visited Oklahoma," he says, "and I really kind of liked it. Barry Switzer and Larry Lacewell—who were OU assistant coaches then—met me when I got off the plane and took me on a tour of the campus.

"Actually, they had just hired Jim Mackenzie, so Switzer and Lacewell had never been on the campus, either. It was the first time for all of us, and we took the tour together."

Looking back, McKay acknowledges the rationale of the argument about how a kid could get lost at a big school like UT. A lot of them did.

"There were no scholarship limits then," he says, "and I remember that there were 13 quarterbacks in my recruiting class. I think we had about 50 guys coming in. All told, they had 11 teams out there—125 guys.

"With the situation like it is today, I guess there's a mindset that guys from the lower classifications—the small towns—aren't going to get recruited by Division I-A teams. But it was a different time then, and there were a lot of us from small towns on scholarship—me, Ted Koy, Forrest Wiegand, Denny Aldridge, a lot of others.

"But I know that I played with a lot of guys on that 1969 team who probably wouldn't get into school today."

McKay notes, "a lot of guys didn't last, but those of us who did, maybe it was just the backbone that we had. Seeing if we could survive with the best was why we came there."

His college education began quickly, McKay says, on the practice field.

"With all those people out there," he says, "I quickly learned that I had not been recruited to offer my input on how things should be run. I was there to do what I was told to do.

"If you were upset about something they told you to do, well, they really didn't care. There were rows of guys standing around waiting to take your place."

Out of this was forged a team that reached the Cotton Bowl when McKay was a junior and won a national championship when he was a senior.

McKay is not inclined toward words like *invincible*, saying simply that, "We just went out and did our job, and we were good at it."

But he probably wouldn't object to *awesome*.

Sometimes the Longhorns were so good that it almost became comical.

"In 1968 when we reached the Cotton Bowl, we were playing Tennessee," he says. "This was a team with a defense that had two All-America linebackers and an All-America defensive back. The first series, we basically ran the same thing every play until we scored.

"They closed up to stop us, and on the first play of the second series, Cotton Speyrer was so wide open he looked like he was fielding a punt when James Street threw him a [78-yard] touchdown pass.

"There were games back then where we could have scored 100 points if Coach Royal had left the first team in, the way a lot of them do today. But in those days we cleared the bench.

"For a long time in the 1969 season, the second-team guys had more minutes of playing time than we did, because we beat people so easily. It looked like they were going to have enough playing time to earn a letter, and we weren't.

"There was one game late in the year where we were so far ahead, there was a running back who had come in with our class and stuck with the team, but he never played because he was so far down the depth chart. He got in at the end of that game, and I remember Coach Royal saying, 'Run him until he scores or they stop him.'

"He didn't play much, but he can always say he scored a touchdown for a team that won the national championship."

There was one game, at the end, that wasn't that easy.

"In those days," McKay says, "when we would play a 'showdown' game against Arkansas or a Cotton Bowl game against Notre Dame, I tended to just look at it as another football game. Wipe away all the hype, and it's still just two teams out there trying to beat each other, and you still have to do your job.

"But now I have to admit that sometimes the significance of a game like that is lost on guys who are 21 or 22 at the time. Looking back, that Arkansas game does seem like something almost magical—especially since people are still writing about it, and the two teams had a great reunion last year.

"I guess I knew it was a big deal when my folks drove up for the game, and they wouldn't sell them any gas in Arkansas. They had to go back to Oklahoma to get gas."

But recalling the day in 1966 when he sat in front of a TV set with a sour expression on his face, McKay says the greatest thing about the 1969 national championship showdown with Arkansas is that it didn't end in a tie.

"That was one thing I loved about Coach Royal," he says. "Whenever it came up, he always said, 'Every time we play, we go out there to win or lose. We don't play for a tie.' If you do that, it was all just a waste of time. He lost a crucial game to Arkansas five years before that by going for two and the win [and failing] instead of kicking the point for the tie."

And on that day, the man who had likened a tie to "kissing your sister" plugged a two-point conversion play into the game plan to make sure somebody left with a national championship.

"But of course," McKay says, "the thing that really saved us that day was our defense. Anytime you lose the ball five times on turnovers and only give up 14 points to the No. 2 team in the nation, you've got one hell of a defense."

A top-round draft pick, McKay played six years with the Cleveland Browns—during which time he met his wife, Donna—and finished playing three years with New England.

"It was just the topping on the cake," he says. "My first year in Cleveland, the biggest problem I had was stifling the urge to ask for autographs. I got people in my locker room like Leroy Kelly and Bill Nelson, and every game I'm lining up against people like Bob Lilly, Merlin Olsen, and Deacon Jones. It was the ultimate schoolboy's dream come true."

He and Donna have been married for 29 years and, he says, she's pretty much become a certified Texan. Their son Josh, 26, is in the construction business in Austin. They also take trips to Union City, Pennsylvania, to visit Jill, 32—Donna's daughter by a previous marriage—who has two children and runs some sawmills with her husband.

"When I left pro football," he says, "we came back down here because we had a house in Austin. I was looking for something to do, and I thought about coaching. But we talked about it and realized it would have to be high school, because in college or pro, you have to move too much. Our son was born the last year I was in New England, and we wanted him to grow up in one place.

"So when I was offered a job here in the tire business, I took it. I worked briefly for another company, and I've worked for the last 23 years for a company called GCR here in Austin. Mostly we sell the big earth-moving stuff, along with some truck tires.

"Basically they pay me to travel around Texas and talk to my friends. I see a lot of my old teammates, and I go out to West Texas and go hunting and fishing with old friends of mine.

"I don't have family out there anymore—my parents moved to Anchorage, Alaska, and worked on the pipeline after my youngest brother got out of high school in 1970. When they retired, they came back and settled in Mason. My dad died in 1996, but mom is still there in Mason going strong at 76."

After two shoulder operations while he was at Texas, McKay got out of pro ball with a bad knee, among other things. He has since had knee replacement surgery.

"My doctor started telling me when I was about 36 or 37 that I needed it," he says. "I always said, 'No way, I'm too young.' And he said, 'You'll be in some day.'

"Sure enough, when I was about 40, I went in and asked for it. I feel a lot better now, and I do pretty much what I want physically."

On the job, McKay says he still travels "about 4,000 or 5,000 miles per month, but that's down from what it used to be. I've covered an area from Nevada to Arkansas, but a lot of it is in Texas, where I see my friends a lot."

With the new regulations that followed 9/11, McKay says he has virtually abandoned air travel.

"It's just gotten to be too much of a hassle," he says. "It's just simpler to drive. In fact, we even drive when we go to Pennsylvania to visit my stepdaughter and her family.

"But overall, life is good. I'd really be hard-pressed to find a better deal than I've got now. I'm just scared they're gonna catch me one of these days and make me take what I've got coming to me."

Where Have You Gone?

DAVID McWILLIAMS

On the Monday in September 1996 that David McWilliams noticed the small trace of blood in the bowl, it was as if he had been whisked back 40 years through time to Fulton Junior High School.

And suddenly, the words of "Big Bill" Anderson came flooding back into his memory—

"If any of you ever see blood in your urine or stool, you let me know. Real quick."

A junior high school coach, Anderson had made that speech long ago to a group of youngsters in Cleburne—most of whom had probably deleted it from memory by the next home room period.

Fortunately, one of them never forgot it.

"Right then, after all those years, it popped into my head," McWilliams says. "The next day I went to see a doctor."

An examination was done, tests were run. That night, the doctor called and said, "It doesn't look good. I'm waiting for the lab results."

Thursday morning he called and said, "It's cancer. You need to come in."

Monday—a week to the day—McWilliams was in surgery, having 13 inches of his colon removed.

The operation was successful, and McWilliams then went through 32 radiation treatments and six months of chemotherapy.

The chemo, he says, was a breeze. Never got sick, never lost a hair.

"The radiation was tough," he said. "I was down to about 168 pounds when I started eating again."

In retaliation, he gave it the full McWilliams treatment.

"One day when I was lying there and they were painting me for the radiation," he says, "I told the girl to paint a flower on my butt.

"Then the next time they redid it, I told them to be sure and put the flower back on, because it seemed to be working pretty well."

DAVID McWILLIAMS
Hgt: 5-11 • Wgt: 186 • Hometown: Cleburne

Years played: 1961-1963
Positions: Center, defensive guard
Highlights: 1963: captain, two-way starter on the
national championship team

Everything seems to be working well these days for McWilliams, who enjoys his job as executive director of the T Association, extending a connection with his alma mater that has been almost a lifelong pursuit.

He also has regular medical checkups, which have produced no evidence of any further problem. But McWilliams's sense of good fortune extends a bit beyond the obvious.

When the cancer was discovered, it had been nearly five years since the December day in 1991 when he lost his job as Texas' head football coach—after a five-year tenure that produced one Southwest Conference title but fell short of the overall progress that McWilliams and others had hoped for.

"There's always a lot of pressure in that job, but it was getting worse," he says. "One day I came home and my daughter, Summer, was sitting in front of the TV set, and she looked up and said, 'Daddy, there's a show on TV that says you're going to be fired. Does that mean Santa won't come this year?'"

McWilliams sat his daughter down and explained that no matter what, Santa would arrive on time. But he shared the frustration of the fans and the administration and in the official parlance resigned for the good of the program.

"I was just discouraged," he says. "I was thinking that this is my school, I've tried hard, and I think I've done a good job recruiting and graduating these kids, but the results are disappointing and I am not getting it done, and it's time for me to step down."

The saving grace was the offer of a fund-raising job from athletic director DeLoss Dodds, which McWilliams eventually accepted.

"I went home and felt sorry for myself for a few days and thought about maybe going somewhere else to coach," he says. "But I realized there wasn't anyplace I wanted to go, and I didn't want to start over in coaching, and Texas was still my school."

So McWilliams gave up something he loved—and maybe saved his life.

"When you're a coach," he says, "you just never seem to have time to take care of your health and a lot of other things. You're always too focused on the job. Coaches don't have time to worry about being sick. They often have heart attacks because they ignored the warning signs.

"When I was going through the surgery, the doctors kept telling me that it's very rare for blood to show up at that early stage. Usually you don't have blood until later, when the condition is far more advanced.

"I don't know why that trace of blood appeared, but I must have had an angel on my shoulder. The thing that amazes me is that I got something done about it immediately. If I had been off coaching somewhere, I probably would have tried to ignore it—until it was too late.

"Anyway, it puts some things in perspective. If you think it's tough going home and telling your kids you may be fired, think what it's like to tell them you may die of cancer."

Another storm weathered by a man who grew up in Cleburne, Texas, in the full certainty that probably nothing in life would ever come easy.

His father, Dennis McWilliams, quit school in the eighth grade and went to work for the railroad to support his mother and four younger siblings after his father died during the Depression.

"He lived a hard life," McWilliams says. "He would keep something like 25 cents a week for himself and give the rest to his mother. By the time I was born in 1942, he was off fighting in World War II.

"Then one day my mother got a letter saying he was missing in action. What had happened was that he and his squad were fighting some SS troops in some small town in France, and he was up on the top of a building shooting at the Germans.

"So pretty soon they just rolled a tank in and blew the building apart. My father was lying in the middle of the street with blood spurting out of his leg like a hydrant until a German doctor came along and put a clamp on it and saved him from bleeding to death."

Captured by the Germans, Dennis McWilliams was soon liberated by the advancing Allies, a sequence in which he was obliged to convince two doctors—one German, one American—not to cut off his leg.

"When he came back from the war, frankly he had a real hard time doing anything for a long while," McWilliams says. "For several years he had one job after another but just couldn't get it together.

"About the only times he seemed to really be at peace were the nights when he would go down and lie on a sandbar in the Brazos River—just trying to forget the war and straighten himself out."

Finally, he did. He eventually landed a job as the Johnson County veterans service officer and then later became the county tax assessor-collector, a job he held for 26 years.

"My dad was a great person, and he had the kind of personality where he was just good at dealing with people," McWilliams says. "People would come into his office mad as hell about their taxes and walk out a little while later laughing and joking with him."

McWilliams's mother, Ginny, was a slightly different package.

"She was a flaming redhead with a personality to match," he says. "She was a very outgoing—and often outspoken—person who enjoyed people and would usually speak her mind. She would get so excited at football games that she would be beating on the people around her with her game program.

"She was very high strung and continually struggled with high blood pressure. When I was born, they told her not to have another child for five years. My little brother finally came along when I was eight."

As a youth, McWilliams never took it for granted that he would go to college.

"Nobody else in my family ever had, and I knew we couldn't really afford it," he says. "I thought about maybe getting a job after high school and working my way through TCU. But it was certainly not out of the question that I would wind up like so many other guys in Cleburne—get out of high school, go off for a few years in the service, then come back, and go to work in the Santa Fe shops."

Cindy and David McWilliams (seated) with Hunter, Corby, Dennis, Clarissa, and Summer (*Photo courtesy of the McWilliams family*)

But in 1959 McWilliams was a two-way star on a Cleburne team that battled Breckenridge to a 20-20 tie in a famous 3-A state title game, and scholarship offers began arriving. He eventually chose Texas, which was pleased to sign a strapping 190-pounder who could play center and either linebacker or a defensive line position.

"In the summer, I got a job breaking rocks," he says, "and I also went down to Baton Rouge and played in something called the Wig Wam Wise Men of the World All-Star Game.

"When I showed up at Texas weighing 172 that fall, I'm not real sure they knew who I was. Funny thing is, in the whole four years at Texas I never regained all that weight. I finally got up to about 186 as a senior."

Which led to some interesting encounters on the field. As a sophomore playing against Mississippi in the Cotton Bowl, McWilliams was informed by massive Rebel tackle Jim Dunaway that he wouldn't even have been allowed to go out for football at Ole Miss. But Texas won the game.

As a senior, he was confronted by Oklahoma All-American Ralph Neely, who said, "What you are is a railroad track, and what I am is a train." But it was the Longhorns who rolled over the Sooners en route to a national championship.

McWilliams was one of the captains on that 1963 team, which emphatically stamped itself as the national champion with a 28-6 rout of second-ranked Navy in the Cotton Bowl.

It was the last football game McWilliams ever played. And unquestionably, the hardest.

Four days before the Cotton Bowl, at age 46, Ginny McWilliams suffered a massive stroke and finally lost a lifelong battle. As a Christmas present to her family, she had promised to go in for a complete medical checkup after the New Year.

"I was in a team meeting when I saw coach [Darrell] Royal at the door, motioning for me," McWilliams says. "I just asked him, 'Is it my mom or my dad?' He said, 'Your dad's on the phone.'

"By that time, he had already called a Texas alum who owned a private plane and arranged to have me flown home immediately.

"I got home quickly, but my mom was in a coma and never came out. When she died, I called Scott Appleton, my roommate, and asked him to let everyone know. Coach Royal called back and said that playing in the game was up to me and that if I didn't feel like I could go through with it, everybody would understand.

"I finally told my dad I was going to play because I thought she would want me to. I figured she had the best seat in the house and would be beating on the other angels with her program. The funeral was two days before the game, and after the service I told Coach Royal I would play."

McWilliams played an outstanding game and then considered staying home with his father.

"But he said, 'You can't help me—the best thing you can do is go back and finish and get a degree, because it's what she wanted.'

"Later, when I walked across that stage, it was probably a more emotional moment for me and my dad than the funeral was. We just stood there and hugged and cried, thinking about her."

Along with a degree in mathematics, McWilliams left Texas in the growing stages of a strong lifelong friendship with Royal.

"I played for him, and I learned a lot from him," McWilliams says. "He was a great help to me in my coaching career and in my life. What he did for me when my mother died is something I have never forgotten.

"Mostly what I got from him was not Xs and Os. It was more about the way he handled people. You learn a lot from him that doesn't have anything to do with football."

It was also Royal who told McWilliams about an opening for an assistant coach at Abilene High, which McWilliams took in 1964.

"It's funny—I had a degree in mathematics, but I hadn't given that much thought to what I would do after college," McWilliams says. "I was just kind of hanging around looking for something to happen when [Royal] told me about that job, and I decided to take it.

"Then one of my professors came around and told me about a really good opportunity opening up with a brand new company that was just getting started.

"I asked him what the name of the company was, and he said, 'International Business Machines.'

"I have to admit I've given that some thought over the years, but I'd already decided to try coaching."

McWilliams stayed in Abilene for six seasons, the last four as head coach. In January 1970, he took Royal up on an offer to return to Texas as freshman line coach. He would spend the next 16 seasons as a UT assistant under Royal and then Fred Akers.

While in Abilene he also became acquainted with a cheerleader named Cindy Hacker. He was so taken with her that he avoided her whenever possible and rarely spoke around her.

"That was because of Coach Royal," he says, laughing. "One of the things he told me was that getting involved with a student is a real quick way to get yourself fired."

But when she returned to Abilene to enroll at McMurry College (now University) the following year, the two began dating.

"Her dad was in the service, and the family moved back to Iowa when she got out of high school," McWilliams says. "Then in the fall of 1966, he called and told her she had to come back because they couldn't afford it anymore. So I said, 'Why don't we get married?'

"I met her dad the afternoon of the wedding and met her mom at the reception. We've been married 37 years, and her folks live in Austin now, and we've become as close as you could imagine."

The couple has four children: Dennis, 33; Corby, 31—who narrowly missed being named after Diron Talbert and is instead named after Corby Robertson; Hunter, 23; and Summer, 20.

In 1986, T Jones hired McWilliams as the head coach at Texas Tech, which had gone through seven straight losing seasons. He engineered a quick turnaround: The team went 7-4 and accepted a bid to the Independence Bowl.

But by the time it got there, McWilliams was no longer the coach. At the end of the season, Texas fired Akers and Dodds hired McWilliams as his replacement.

"It really surprised me, because I didn't think they were going to fire Fred," McWilliams says. "I was driving to the store and Corby was in the car, and they came on the radio and said the UT Athletic Council was meeting. Corby said, 'What do you think they'll do?' and I said, 'I don't think they're going to do anything.'

"When we came back out of the store, they were saying on the radio that Fred had been fired, and Corby said, 'Now what are you going to do?' I said, 'I'm not going to do anything.'

"We got home and Cindy said, 'DeLoss just called.'"

Tech fans reacted bitterly, but anyone taking a cursory glance at McWilliams's life could have easily predicted it. Ever since he left Cleburne High School, the Texas connection has been strong.

"It was a hard decision, but I did what was best for my family," he says. "I've never been one to look back, and my only real regret is for the flak that T took over it. It wasn't a matter of me wanting to leave Tech; that was never what it was about.

"I just came home."

He has been there ever since, even though it ultimately meant giving up his coaching career.

"I enjoy my job with the T Association, because it puts me in contact with coaches and players again, and that's what I like," he said. "Coach Royal and I often travel together, and I'm healthy and feel great.

"I couldn't ask for it to be any better."

Where Have You Gone?

RICHARD OCHOA

It is now known as the University of Louisiana at Monroe, but more than half a century ago, it turned out to be the promised land for a homesick kid from Laredo.

When Richard Ochoa arrived there in 1948, the school was known as Northeast Louisiana, and he wasn't even sure where it was—only that one of his seven older brothers went to school there.

"That's how it all started," Ochoa says. "My brother was in school there, and he talked to the football coach about me, and they offered me a scholarship to come there and play football.

"It seemed like a long way away, and I was pretty much bewildered and homesick, but the coach there helped me a lot. I think he gave me a backbone and some confidence, and I matured a lot at Northeast."

Now a retired pharmaceutical rep living the good life in El Paso, Ochoa recalls his one year in Monroe as being "fun"—although today's average high school recruit would be a bit put off.

"There was no athletic dorm," he says. "We slept in the stadium on bunk beds. The school was about three blocks away, and we walked to class. There was also a cafeteria where we got our meals, and we also got our books. Other than that, we got $8 per month laundry money.

"That was our scholarship, and I was very grateful to have it."

Ochoa, however, was about to take a step up.

"At the end of that year," he says, "I had an opportunity to visit LSU and Tulane, and I also had some feelers from Houston and Texas A&M. When I visited Tulane, coach Henry Frnka put me through a tryout and then offered me a four-year scholarship. I accepted and then went home.

"My brother had now transferred to Texas to pursue an engineering degree, and during the summer I was contacted by Texas coach Blair Cherry. I had accepted a scholarship at Tulane and signed a letter of intent with the Southeastern Conference, but then I got to a crossroads and changed my mind.

RICHARD OCHOA
Hgt: 6-2 • Wgt: 195 • Hometown: Laredo

Years played: 1950-1952
Position: Fullback
Highlights: 1952: All-SWC, leading rusher (819 yards), Cotton Bowl
MVP (108 yards)

"I disappointed Tulane and transferred to Texas, my reasoning being that since I was from Texas and my brother was enrolled in the university, it was probably the better place for me. I had good grades and could have gone either way, but I preferred the Texas offer.

"Of course, they probably would have never heard of me if Tulane hadn't recruited me. Anyway, things worked out pretty well."

After sitting out a year, Ochoa played sparingly as a sophomore on the 1950 team that won the Southwest Conference title. In 1951, he was the backup fullback behind Byron Townsend, the Longhorns' leading All-America candidate, and seemed destined for only occasional duty.

But in the SMU game, Townsend suffered a horrific injury that ended his UT career.

"It was really horrible," Ochoa says. "As I recall, he took the opening kickoff and kind of moved out to the side before turning upfield. He had his leg planted and seemed to stop for a minute to let a tackler miss, and the guy hit his leg and upended him. It basically just ripped part of the buttocks from the hipbone.

"I was standing on the sideline, and the coach put his arms around me and said, 'Okay, you're in.'"

Ochoa responded with 139 yards on 28 carries, and a star career was launched. Or as Townsend later remarked, "The guy they put in to replace me nearly made All-American in one afternoon."

In 1952, Ochoa was the leading rusher on another SWC championship team— one on which the entire backfield was named All-Conference.

"Ed Price was the coach by then," he says, "and he had us running that Split-T offense that Bud Wilkinson had been raising so much havoc with up at Oklahoma. We had a great backfield, and by the end of the season, we were pretty good running that offense."

Ochoa finished with 927 yards, including 108 in the Cotton Bowl victory over Tennessee, and is 22nd on the all-time UT list with 1,494 yards in basically less than two seasons. He still has the game ball he was awarded from the 1952 TCU game and is also in UT's Hall of Honor.

On June 28, 1953, with teammate Gib Dawson acting as best man, Ochoa married Marilyn Hampton, a former UT coed from Dallas.

"We met while we were going to school there," he says, "and all these years since, I've been in the pharmaceutical business, and she's been teaching school. Now we're both retired and enjoying life."

The couple has two children: Elizabeth Ann (Beth Ann) Steele, 47, who has a master's degree in special education, is an El Paso schoolteacher , and has a daughter, Audrey; and Richard Jr., 45, who is in the construction business in San Francisco.

Coming out of UT, Ochoa was drafted by the Giants—but as usual in the Korean War era, it was put on hold while he completed military service.

"I had a commission and did two years in the Air Force," he says. "I spent most of it in the intelligence service.

"When I got out, the Giants contacted me about coming to camp and trying out. As I recall, they offered to pay my way to camp, pick up my expenses, and then if I made the team, sign me to a contract for about $6,000."

So Ochoa went back to Plan A.

"When I graduated from Texas, I had applied for medical school," he says, "but it got put on hold because of the military service. So after I got out, I reapplied in several places. Galveston said no, Baylor said no, but Southwestern Medical School was just getting started and they gave me one of the five alternate positions. But I never got the acceptance.

"I went in for an interview, and it seemed to me that all the questions were pretty basic. But I never got into Southwestern Medical School.

"Looking back on it later, I remember one question about how I was going to afford medical school: What was my plan? I didn't have one, and I think that question carried a lot of weight."

And so, for the next move—

"Life goes on," Ochoa says. "I was married and had a daughter. My father-in-law, Mr. Hamilton, owned several dry cleaning businesses in Dallas, and he offered me a chance to come in and work with him. So that's what I did for about the next six or seven years."

But as it turned out, Ochoa's future lay elsewhere—both professionally and geographically.

"Finally I interviewed with a pharmaceutical company, and I've been in that business ever since, as a sales rep. The first one I talked to was Upjohn. They hired me in Dallas and then sent me to Wichita Falls, and I stayed there two years, working for them."

But he was soon interviewing with a new company, for a chance to move to a new location.

"I met a lot of really good people in Wichita Falls and particularly the smaller towns around there like Vernon and Iowa Park," he says. "When I went into Childress and they found out I had played football with T Jones, I was the toast of the town.

"And in Wichita Falls, I ran into several doctors who had gone to UT, and I wound up doing good business with them. There was one who was particularly friendly and rented us a really nice house he owned in a real good neighborhood.

"But there was—an overall culture there in which, for one of the few times in my life, I felt uncomfortable as a Hispanic. I finally just felt I needed to move to an area that was better suited for me."

This eventually led Ochoa to Roche Laboratories, a U.S. division of a Swiss company known as Hoffman-LaRoche. There, he found a home.

"I interviewed in Fort Worth with a guy named Jim Peabody from Roche Labs, and he said he might soon have an opening in El Paso or Albuquerque, and I said either would be fine with me. We finally settled on El Paso.

"So I became their sales rep for the area—selling their products throughout the Southwest, eastern New Mexico, and El Paso. That was in 1967, and 30 years later I retired.

"That was a job I really loved. There were three of us covering that area—one guy was in Odessa, one in Albuquerque, and I was in El Paso, so we were pretty spread out.

"The real satisfying thing was that it was a real quality company, first class in every way. There was never any of this stuff you have with some corporations where they're constantly revising your job or coming up with quotas or new marketing techniques or any of those kind of management games you see now.

"They just depended on you to be their representative out in your area, and they pretty much left you alone to do your job. They just wanted you to keep it growing and keep it going, and I was pretty much on my own.

"I retired with a 401K, a pension, great benefits. It is truly a company that cares about its people.

"My wife also retired after 30 years of teaching third grade, but she still runs into former students here and there. One day a young man wearing a uniform showed up, and when my wife answered the door, he introduced himself. She had taught him in third grade and now he was about to graduate from the Air Force Academy.

"He was home for a visit, and he said, 'Mrs. Ochoa, I just wanted to come by and say thank you for being the greatest teacher I ever had and for all you did for me.' That was really something."

As for Ochoa, one of his proudest achievements was being recently inducted into the El Paso Hall of Fame, despite the fact that he's not a native.

"I guess they figure I've been here long enough," he says.

For the Ochoas, life in retirement means taking trips—a lot of them.

"We travel, mainly," he says. "We go up to Ruidoso, go skiing with the kids. We're going to take a river cruise through Europe this year. We went a year ago and went to London and all through Europe. Then Grandmother took Audrey on an educational tour of Europe last spring when she graduated.

"We're going out to Vegas pretty soon. Then down to St. Thomas. It's really wonderful to be able to find time to do this and be healthy enough and able to afford it. It's a good life."

Included among the exotic locales the couple has visited is one that Ochoa knew long ago.

"We went down to Laredo," he says. "It's been a long time since I was there. The only relatives I have left there are second and third generation. We went by the old house. My dad used to have fruit trees, pecan trees—they've cut a lot of them down to build another house on the property.

"Looking at the old house, it's like, how in the world did eight kids and two adults come out of there? It's not that big. My dad, he worked 32 years for the railroad—the kids, we all turned out pretty well.

"It's funny. If I hadn't gone off to Northeast all those years ago, I probably would have lived my whole life in Laredo."

Where Have You Gone?

RANDY PESCHEL

A s a wee lad, Randy Peschel once confided to his mother that his greatest dream was to someday stand in a victorious locker room and have the President of the United States walk in and ask to meet him.

His mother tenderly caressed his cheek and replied, "Yeah, right kid—eat your carrots."

Okay, so the dream is a bit contrived, but the scenario became a reality.

It occurred late in the day on December 6, 1969, when Richard Nixon walked into the Texas locker room following one of the most climactic battles in college football history, in which the Longhorns won a national championship with a 15-14 victory over Arkansas.

Nixon joined coach Darrell Royal on a podium, made some congratulatory remarks to coach and team, and then said to Royal, "I want to meet that boy who caught the pass."

Aha. That would be young Peschel, who was instantly summoned to the podium.

"So, I got to shake hands with the president," he says. "Kind of a neat way to end the day."

He performed this ceremony, of course, little realizing at the time that his 15 minutes of fame would eventually stretch past 35 years and counting. The events of that day have since been the subject of several books and countless newspaper and magazine articles. Last year the two squads even held a reunion in Fayetteville.

It was the game of the year, and in retrospect probably the game of the century—the most famous college football game ever played. And in the fourth quarter, the tide dramatically turned on the 44-yard pass Peschel caught from James Street to set up the winning touchdown.

It is a moment that has followed Peschel, 56, throughout his life.

Even today, total strangers stop dead in their tracks when the name is mentioned. They stare at him in awe.

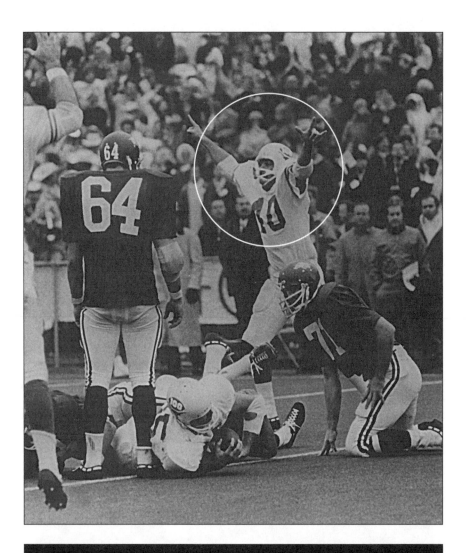

RANDY PESCHEL
Hgt: 6-1 • Wgt: 195 • Hometown: Austin

Years played: 1967-1969
Positions: Wingback, tight end
Highlights: Tight end on the 1969 national championship team;
caught 44-yard pass that set up the winning touchdown in
The Great Shootout with Arkansas

"Peschel?" they will say. "*The* Randy Peschel? The man who ..."

Oh, stop it. You people sound like the president.

"I can't believe that 35 years later people are still talking about it," he says, laughing. "That absolutely amazes me. It was just a football game, but so many people seem to remember it so well."

At the very least, it was a grand finish for Peschel, who at that point had one game left—against Notre Dame in the Cotton Bowl—in his career. For a hometown boy who throughout his career could have been considered a victim of circumstances, becoming a lifetime Longhorn legend was a just and fitting climax.

Recruited out of high school as a quarterback, he gladly switched positions—to wingback—for an opportunity to play. Then in his junior year he seemingly became victim to a phenomenon—the Wishbone.

Many are those who have one day discovered that they have disappeared from the depth chart. Peschel one day discovered that his *position* had disappeared.

He was moved to wide receiver as a backup to one of the best in the country—Cotton Speyrer—with little chance of moving up. He then became the backup tight end behind another large talent, Deryl Comer. It was only through Comer's knee injury, which forced him to miss most of the 1969 season, that Peschel got his chance.

And it all began with home-baked cookies and a visit from Edith.

"I was recruited by a few people out of high school," he says, "but growing up in Austin, I was pretty much leaning toward Texas.

"Then when Coach Royal came to the door for the recruiting visit, he had Edith, [his wife], with him. We were all amazed. My mother had made cookies, and Darrell and Edith raved about them, and after that I was definitely set on Texas. Somewhere in there, I think Coach Royal may have mentioned that it was Edith's first recruiting trip."

When he got to Texas, Peschel encountered a wider world.

"When I was a freshman, I was one of seven quarterbacks," he says, "and after the first practice, it was obvious that that was not going to be my position. I welcomed the chance to move to wingback."

As a sophomore, in 1967, he was a starter.

"We were in the I Formation, and I was basically a glorified blocker," he says. "But it was a thrill just to play in a backfield with Bill Bradley, Chris Gilbert, and Linus Baer.

"I was thrilled just playing wingback—caught some passes, even threw one [incomplete]. But when they switched offenses, I realized I just needed to play whatever position they told me to play.

"I always prided myself as being an athlete—being able to play a lot of different positions. When they moved me out there behind Cotton, I knew I wasn't going to see much playing time, but if it worked, fine. It's a team game. I accepted that.

"Even when Deryl got hurt, I had no idea I would be the starting tight end. I assumed they would move someone else in there. But as it turns out, I was fortunate, and the rest, as they say, is history."

Indeed it is.

As for the play that so enthralled Nixon and others, it was less a pass than a heat-seeking missile that shattered the dreams of an entire state.

When it left the sideline, rattling around in the brain of James Street, it was a weird play called Right 53 Veer Pass. When it settled into Peschel's arms moments later, it was a miracle.

Sitting at fourth and three at their 43 in a Wishbone offense, the chances that the Longhorns would throw deep were comparable to the notion that Communist China would become Baptist. Given the chance that Texas might throw the deep pass, the only person on the field less likely than Peschel to be the primary receiver was Frank Broyles.

Nevertheless, when Street reached the huddle with his "Boys, you ain't gonna believe this," line, he was speaking directly to Peschel in a peculiar way.

"He was saying, 'Peschel, don't look at me,' and he was looking at Cotton while he was calling the play, because he believed [Arkansas] was looking into our huddle, trying to determine who would get the ball on the next play," Peschel says. "He also told me that if I couldn't get deep, to come back toward him so he could throw a pass for the first down."

It was an instruction Street soon regretted—fearing that Peschel might turn back, and he would overthrow him—but he needn't have worried. Peschel ignored it.

"When I got into my stance," he says, "I planted my foot to go deep. I never considered anything else. I was going all the way."

The nature of the play—the last thing on earth anyone expected—was, of course, the reason why Royal called it. But the decision was also bolstered by information Peschel had given the coaching staff at halftime: The Arkansas defensive backs were charging up hard on the option and the deep pass might be open.

The play was designed to draw the defense in to stop the option and spring the tight end open on a deep route. When the ball reached Peschel, he seemed well covered by two defenders, a situation he attributes to his speed.

"They definitely bit on the veer fake and came up," he says, laughing. "But with my speed, they caught up to me by the time the ball got there."

In most accounts, it is described as a difficult—even miraculous—catch by a receiver fighting off near-lockdown double coverage. That isn't quite the way Peschel remembers it.

"Actually, it was an easy catch," he says. "It was a perfectly thrown pass that just dropped right into my hands with a pinpoint touch. The amazing thing about it was that when I looked up, I saw 10 fingers reaching for the ball. I was running, and I just watched the ball miss those fingers by about eight to 10 inches, and I caught it."

Two plays later, Texas scored the winning touchdown, and about 45 minutes after that, Peschel and the chief executive were pals. By that time, of course, he had already convinced his sweetheart, Sue, to marry him. And amazingly, he still had a ring to give her.

The Peschel family: (back row) Sue, Randy, Randy Jr., and Patrick; (front row) Melissa, Ella, Ali, and Lucas (*Photo courtesy of the Peschel family*)

"Okay, it was not the brightest thing I ever did," he says, recalling the odyssey of the diamond wedding ring he took with him to College Station for the annual Texas–A&M bash over the Thanksgiving weekend. Arriving for the game, he promptly stashed it in a safe place—in his shaving kit on the top shelf of an *open* locker.

It was actually still there when he returned several hours later after the Horns had bashed the Aggies. He took it back to Austin, where he eventually presented it to Sue at the fountain in front of The Tower—lit orange for a UT win.

"We met when I first started in college and she was still in high school," he says. "We started dating in 1966 and got married in 1970."

It was also in 1970, in the spring, that Peschel made a decision he has regretted ever since. An outfielder on the baseball team throughout his UT career, he abruptly quit in his senior season.

"It had always been my dream to play baseball in the major leagues," he says, "and I had played in a program that reached the College World Series the two previous years.

"But I had just a horrible year as a senior. Nothing was going right, and it was like every time I went up to the plate, I didn't know what to do. So I wound up quitting. I loved baseball, but at the time we had just won the national championship in football, and I wasn't having a good [baseball] season, and I guess I just didn't think I would miss it.

"It's been the greatest regret of my life."

It also left Peschel wondering what to do with the rest of his life, but he soon got a helping hand from prominent UT booster Frank Denius.

"He was the director of a bank, and he helped me get an interview," Peschel says, "and so I went to work at what was then Capital National Bank while I was finishing school. Then I stayed on full time and got into the real estate department right off the bat.

"I stayed there seven years, doing real estate loans, and then moved to City National Bank for two years, doing the same thing.

"Then I went out to do some building on my own, and eventually, with a partner, bought an existing floor and roof truss manufacturing plant in San Marcos. We still lived here in Austin, and I just commuted down there, and I did that from 1979 to 1986.

"But when the economy went down in the 1980s, it was a real rocky time for a lot of people, and the market for what we were doing pretty much dried up. In 1986 I got back into banking with a startup bank, Cattleman's State Bank, which actually did quite well.

"I stayed there for five years and then went to work for one of my builder customers—Legend Homebuilders—and I was the CFO for eight years until the company shut down in 1999. So I went back to banking."

Peschel is now a vice president at Compass Bank. He and Sue have been married for 34 years and have three children: Ali, 31, is married to Lucas Patterson, who is in commercial real estate in Austin. They have two daughters, Ella and Hattie. Melissa, 27, is a deputy administrator at the Governor's Mansion. She and her husband, attorney Patrick Smith, have a daughter, Mary Carolyn. Randy Jr., 21, is a senior at UT majoring in sports management but Peschel says, "He's working for BLT Construction here in Austin and he loves it, and I think he'll stay in that field."

For the past 10 years, Sue has worked as a secretary-receptionist for her father and brother, both chiropractors.

Regarding the moment that made his name a household word for Longhorn fans, Peschel laughs and says, "It's kind of a shame to do something like that when you're 21 years old and then have it all go downhill from there.

"Seriously, it's really been a lot of fun from time to time. I guess there's hardly a day goes by that someone doesn't ask me about it or that I'm reminded about it— or that sometimes, I just think about it myself.

"It's been fun for my kids, and maybe it will be for my grandchildren. Looking back on my time at UT, I regret the decision to quit baseball, but the rest of it was very positive. I think that as time goes by you have a chance to appreciate it more, and I can't say enough about how much I benefited from my association with Coach Royal and [baseball coach] Cliff Gustafson.

"Business-wise, the 1980s were awful, and I would just as soon not have had the experience. But we came through it, and I have a great family, and there's nothing I would trade for.

"Life is good."

Where Have You Gone?

BEN PROCTER

For Ben Procter, getting to know William Randolph Hearst has become a project of considerable length.

There was a first meeting 35 years ago. Then another in the mid-1970s, and a third a few years later.

Before long, the two were meeting every five years, or whenever Procter—a professor of history at TCU for 44 years—could take a sabbatical.

Eventually he felt he had come to know the famed publisher fairly well.

Hearst, of course, had been long dead by the time this relationship began. Procter's periodic but extensive research was in conjunction with a project he and a fellow scholar had planned for years: a two-volume biography.

A small hitch developed: Due to death in the family and personal illness, Procter's partner was forced to drop out of the project, leaving him to finish both volumes himself.

The first—*William Randolph Hearst: The Early Years, 1863-1910*—was published in 1998 by Oxford University Press. The second, covering the final years of Hearst's life (1910-1951), should be released "in a year or two," Procter says.

"One of the key points here," he says, "is that Hearst's life lasted 88 years.

"One of the key points for me is that if I ever do another biography, it will be of William Barrett Travis, who died at age 27 at the Alamo."

Don't bet on it. A Phi Beta Kappa graduate at UT with a doctorate from Harvard, Procter has left a long trail of distinguished scholarship behind him, and the second Hearst volume is the 12th book he has authored or collaborated on.

But long before all of that began to unfold, he was something else: sure-handed and swift, one of the greatest pass receivers in the history of UT or the Southwest Conference.

He caught 43 passes in 1949, establishing a Longhorn single-season standard that stood for 40 years. The next season, he was the leading receiver on a team that

BEN PROCTER
Hgt: 6-1 • Wgt: 195 • Hometown: Austin

Years played: 1948-1950
Position: End
Highlights: Leading receiver for three seasons; caught 43 passes in 1949,
setting a record that stood for 40 years

made a serious run at a national championship. He left behind career records for receptions and yardage that stood for three decades.

As a time perspective, Procter began setting records at UT when Darrell Royal was the quarterback at Oklahoma. By the time his records began to fall, Royal was retired from coaching.

"I was born in Temple, but we moved to Austin when I was 12," he says. "I can still remember sitting in the stands when Noble Doss made 'The Catch' against the Aggies in 1940.

"I went to Austin High, and we had good teams. We beat [Dallas'] Sunset for the state championship in 1942 and got eliminated from the playoffs in 1944 by Port Arthur, which went on to win the state championship.

"We were running the single wing then, and I made All-State—as a center."

After graduation in 1945, Procter spent 15 months in the Navy, as World War II was winding down.

"Part of that time," he says, "I was on the USS *Mississippi*, which had suffered a kamikaze attack back in the spring. Fortunately, I missed it."

Weighing several scholarship offers coming out of the Navy, Procter wound up at Texas. One of his new teammates was Bobby Layne, a man of unusual proclivities.

"Everyone who ever knew him has stories to tell about him," Procter says. "One thing I remember is that he and his buddies on the team loved to play cards. Once when we were scheduled to play a road game at Baylor the next day, they stayed up all night playing poker in the dorm.

"The next morning, they rushed over to the dining hall and ate breakfast, then went back to playing poker. All through the two-hour trip up to Waco, they played poker, with no sleep at all.

"When the game started, all those other guys got gassed pretty quick and weren't much help. But Layne scored two touchdowns, kicked three field goals, and led the team to a 22-7 victory. The most incredible performance I ever saw.

"The following week we played TCU, and for some reason, Layne got to bed at 10 p.m. and got a full night's sleep. The next day we lost, and he said, 'That's the last damn time I go to bed early the night before a game.'"

Procter's career at Texas coincided with the four-year Blair Cherry era.

"He was a smart coach who had won a lot of state titles at Amarillo in the 1930s and then became a UT assistant," Procter says. "When Dana Bible retired, Cherry became the new head coach in 1947. He switched to the T Formation, and he also switched me to end. He was successful, but he took a lot of criticism."

Procter's record-setting 1949 season was due largely to extra work he and quarterback Paul Campbell put in during the summer, and by the time the season started, their timing was infallible. But although the Longhorns averaged nearly 30 points per game, they lost four times—by a total margin of 10 points. Fans were not pleased.

"Every team in the league had great players then," Procter says. "Doak Walker was at SMU, Jess Neely had a powerhouse at Rice. Late in the season we lost by one point to TCU, which was coached by Dutch Meyer.

"He was a fine person—good man, straight arrow. Horrible to have to play against. He always came up with something different, and although his teams often started slowly, by the ninth game of the season they were as tough as any in the nation.

"He threw a nine-man line at us and beat us 14-13. I caught a lot of passes that day, but it didn't help us much."

The Longhorns redeemed themselves in 1950, rolling to a 9-1 season, a SWC title, and a No. 3 national ranking.

Unfortunately, the lone defeat—a 14-13 loss to eventual national champion Oklahoma—set the hounds on Cherry for what proved to be the last time. Leading by six points late in the game, Texas fumbled a punt snap, leading to an easy OU drive for the winning points. Cherry's fan mail was both voluminous and vicious.

At midseason, the Longhorns faced unbeaten SMU—which was led by Kyle Rote, ranked No. 1 in the nation, and had been featured in a cover story in *Life* magazine.

"It was a bloodbath—on both sides," Procter says.

Early in the game, returning to the huddle after running a pass route downfield, he heard someone yell, "Hey, Procter—how's the ticket business?"

"I turned around," he says, "and it was Rote. He was grinning at me because he was in the same business.

"Back then, it wasn't illegal to sell your game tickets. In fact, it was the accepted method by which athletes on scholarship made extra money. Beyond that, you got tuition, room and board, and $10 a month. So they gave you a certain number of tickets. Usually, you could sell six tickets for about $35.

"But that game was so big, I sold two tickets for $50 and two more for $60. Rote was doing the same, and that's why he was grinning."

Late in the game, Procter caught what proved to be the winning touchdown pass, because the extra-point kick put Texas up 21-20. The Longhorns added a safety in the final minute for an upset 23-20 win.

Shortly afterward, Cherry announced his resignation, effective at the end of the season.

"By that time, he had really bad ulcers," Procter said, "and we rarely saw him for the last four games of the season."

Texas won them all and wound up facing Tennessee in the Cotton Bowl.

"Cherry was around for part of the time during preparations," Procter said, "but we basically didn't show up. That last game, we were a great team with a bad attitude, and we lost 20-14."

Afterward, Procter had a pro career that was brief and eventful.

Former House Speaker Jim Wright and Ben Procter. (*Photo courtesy of the Procter family*)

"I was drafted by the Rams," he says. "In the first [exhibition] game I made a diving catch of a pass from Norm Van Brocklin. As I was lying there on the ground, two guys speared me in the back and broke three lumbar vertebrae."

Unable to play for the rest of the season, Procter returned to Texas, completed his master's degree in 1952, and married Phoebe.

"The first time I met her, I asked her for a date," he says. "She informed me that she was still in high school and was only 16 years old, and could not possibly be going out with a college man until she was 17. So I had to wait until her next birthday, and we started dating after that."

They have been married 53 years. A son, Ben Rice Procter, is a 1978 graduate of TCU and spent 13 years working for former House speaker Jim Wright. He is now an attorney in Austin.

For Procter, there was one more fling with pro ball.

"Dick Todd called me and said he was coaching the Washington Redskins and wanted me to play for them," he says. "So I worked out and played one exhibition game where we got beaten really bad by San Francisco.

"Then Dick came around and said that the owner, George Marshall, had decided that every player should go both ways, and I would have to play defensive halfback as well as receiver. I said, 'I can't play that position here. That's ridiculous,' and he told me to try it for just a week, that the idea wouldn't last.

"But I left, and that was the end of my football career. I applied at Harvard and was accepted, and we went up there in August. In September, I read that Dick had resigned as coach of the Redskins."

After completing his doctorate in 1957, Procter originally thought of going back to teach at Texas. But through a personal connection between his father and TCU chancellor M.E. Sadler, he and Phoebe wound up in Fort Worth.

They bought a house on Boyd, near the campus, and have lived on the same street ever since, although they later moved into a larger house a few blocks down the street.

"We bought the house from Lyndon Johnson's sister in 1966," Phoebe says. "She remarked that during the [1964] election, there were Goldwater signs in yards all up and down the street, and the only yards with signs supporting Lyndon were hers, ours, and one other.

"So she asked if we were interested in buying the house, because she didn't want to sell it to a Republican. We've been here ever since."

At TCU, the coaching staff was originally pleased to have its players taking history classes from a former football player. Until two of them flunked.

"When the grades were posted," Procter says, "they came to me and said, 'What do we do now?' And I said, 'Take the course over—from someone else.' But I also had players who were good students."

Whoever showed up in his classes was subjected to a study of history based on an analytical approach, something Procter picked up at Harvard. Students were assigned to compare and contrast conflicting philosophies, different forms of government, opposite sides of crucial historical moments.

"A sample might be to compare the foreign policies of Washington and Jefferson and decide which was best and explain why," he said. "Or review the period between 1763 and 1776 and decide how you would vote—for independence or staying with England?

"At that time, actually, about one-third were patriots, one-third preferred to remain with England, and one-third opted to stay out of it."

As for the Hearst project, Procter's involvement progressed from mild curiosity to fascination.

"In the beginning," Procter says, "I didn't know anything about him except his association with 'yellow journalism' and the fact that he persuaded the government to go to war with Spain to free Cuba in 1898. I was also aware of his long competition with Joseph Pulitzer and his later relationship with the actress Marion Davies. And the mansion that he built in California, San Simeon.

"But I had no in-depth knowledge of him. What I discovered, over many years, is that he was a genius in a lot of ways. I saw something on television the other night that said he built San Simeon as a tribute to his mother. Like hell he did—he built it as a tribute to himself, his genius.

"I certainly can't say I agree with his politics, but in writing about him I have just tried to record what he did, what he thought, how he felt. One thing I discovered above all, is that he was never dull."

Hearst, who took over the *San Francisco Examiner* in 1887 at age 23, virtually remade the newspaper business.

"The first thing he did was reduce the number of columns and increase the size of the print, so people could actually read it," Procter says. "Then he started coming up with one idea after another to make the paper more interesting and get more subscribers.

"He created so many things that have been regular features ever since—the daily weather report, obituaries, crossword puzzles. He began emphasizing news for and about women. He ran coverage of the World Series on the front page.

"He perceived that Americans loved stories about European royalty and also about American royalty—the Vanderbilts, the Rockefellers. He always felt he had the pulse of the American people.

"He created contests: Win a 10-room house in San Francisco. He had contests for kids: Name the best president and explain why, and win a trip to France or Italy.

"He was fascinated with stories of human frailty. He sent reporters out to try to scoop the police on crime stories."

He also began to take increasing liberties with the usual concepts of journalism in the course of his battle with Pulitzer to become the nation's leading publisher.

"He loved printing wild stories to capture the public's attention," Procter says. "In the beginning, his rule was that the stories had to be interesting but with two factual confirmations. Finally it got to the point where they just had to be well written.

"A lot of them were made up, including the stories accusing the Spaniards of sinking the battleship *Maine*, which led to the Spanish-American War. We finally found out in 1976 that the ship sank because a magazine blew up."

In later years, Hearst married Davies and built San Simeon, a fabulous place that Procter has visited several times. Built on a mountaintop, it is an immense mansion with extensive grounds and several cottages, and once included the world's largest zoo.

"He would have dinner parties in a great dining hall where he entertained the rich and famous," Procter says. "The food was served on a huge 16th-century dining table, and guests ranged from film celebrities to George Bernard Shaw and Winston Churchill.

"He was certainly a unique individual, and while this project has entailed far more than I originally envisioned, I think it has been worth the effort."

RENE RAMIREZ

It can probably be said of Rene Ramirez that, at 68, he can look back on a full life that has encompassed its share of adventures and misadventures.

Since leaving the University of Texas in 1960 with a mechanical engineering degree, Ramirez has been successful in three different fields, spending 25 years in the insurance business, another five with Mobil Oil Corp., and the last 16 as a surveyor for the state. He has also owned a car wash, a barbeque restaurant, an ice cream parlor, and two ranches.

He has been married twice, for a total of 45 years, and has nine children.

He spent years moving back and forth between Hebbronville and Austin, once bailed out of a high-profile job because he didn't want to live in Houston, and says he is now happy in McAllen.

He has run for public office and lost and watched a daughter battle leukemia and win.

And he still recalls with great clarity—"I can probably repeat it word for word," he says—the conversation he had in the spring of 1957 with Texas' new head football coach, Darrell Royal. It was not a happy moment.

"It was the spring of my freshman year, so I was there at the beginning of the Darrell Royal era," he says. "When people ask what that was like, I have to say it was probably different for me than for some other guys—because I wasn't supposed to come back."

Ramirez had been an All-State receiver at Class 1-A Hebbronville in 1955, out of a program that had sent quarterback Rode Gonzalez to TCU the previous year.

"I had an uncle, Valentin, who had pitched at Texas A&M in the 1930s, and he only had to say one word and I would have gone there," Ramirez says. "But he let me make up my own mind, and I chose Texas, because I had been a Longhorn fan and they threw the ball quite a bit."

Ramirez got there in the fall of 1956, just in time to watch the program collapse in a 1-9 disaster. Royal was brought in as the new coach, and by the time he conducted his first spring session, Ramirez was feeling a little collapsible himself.

RENE RAMIREZ

Hgt: 6-2 • Wgt: 180 • Hometown: Hobbronville

Years played: 1957-1959
Position: Halfback
Highlights: 1959: All-SWC on a team ranked No. 4 in the nation

In an era when the term *scholarship limits* constituted a foreign tongue, there were prospective new Longhorns all over Travis County, and Ramirez—a 175-pound receiver from a Class 1-A school—was not exactly at the top of the list. He was also having other problems.

"When they tested me as a mechanical engineering major, they said I had a deficiency in physics," he says. "The deficiency was they didn't have physics at my high school, so I had never taken it. So I had to take it that first year at Texas, and it was eating my lunch.

"I went to one of the coaches to see about a tutor, and he said I'd have to see Coach Royal. I really didn't want to, but things were getting worse, and finally I had no choice.

"When I got to his office, the first thing he said to me was, 'Rene, are you thinking about transferring?'

"Well, actually, I was. Gil Steinke at Texas A&I wanted me to transfer over and be his main receiver, because Texas was changing its offense and I hadn't played much on the freshman team anyway. But I didn't want Royal to know that, so I said no.

"And he said, 'Well, we'd like for you to transfer, because frankly you're not going to be much help to us.'

"My heart sank like a rock, and I said, 'But I haven't even had a chance yet.'

"And he said, 'Well, from what we've seen, you're just not a fit,' and I said, 'Coach, if you just give me a chance, I know I can prove myself.' And he said, 'Well, we haven't seen much of you this spring.'

"So I said, 'Coach, I'm gonna stay.'

"He said, 'Well, if you want to stay, I have to tell you that we're going to have two teams, an A team and a B team. The A team will consist of the first four teams and the B team will be the fifth, sixth, seventh, and eighth. You'll be on the B team.'

"I said, 'Coach, I'm staying.'

"He said, 'We're going to work the B team harder.'

"I said, 'Coach, I'm staying.'

"So he finally approved a tutor for me, and as I started to leave, he said, 'Rene, if you work hard, you might be able to move up to the first team. It's all up to you.'"

With the help of a local pharmacist who fed him a milkshake with an egg in it every day, Ramirez was 20 pounds heavier when he came back in the fall, finally dropping back to 183 as a playing weight.

"I started off on the seventh team [as a right halfback]," he says, "but two guys got hurt and another quit and got married, and I moved up to fourth team.

"Then we had a scrimmage and I did well, and Coach Royal moved me up to the third team. We had another scrimmage, and he put me on the second team. So when we opened the season at Georgia, I made the trip.

"Then I sat on the bench all night, even though we won pretty handily. I finally got to play in the last five minutes.

Rene Ramirez (*Photo courtesy of the Ramirez family*)

"On Monday, Coach Royal came around and said, 'Rene, to be honest, I didn't play you last week because I didn't have confidence in you. But when you got in, you played well. You didn't carry the ball, but you blocked well, carried out your fakes, did your job. Get ready to play against Tulane.'

"I had a good game against Tulane and played regularly after that."

As a three-year regular, Ramirez proved extremely useful in the launching of the Royal era.

As a sophomore, when the Longhorns made an amazing turn-around from 1-9 to a Sugar Bowl appearance, he led the team in scoring and all-purpose yards. As a junior, when Texas snapped a six-year losing streak to Oklahoma, he was the team's total offense leader. As a senior, he was an All-Southwest Conference selection helping to lead the Longhorns to the Cotton Bowl.

A versatile player who could run, catch, and throw, he also provided the Longhorns with a unique strength from the right halfback position, because he was left-handed. The halfback pass off the sweep was a favorite Royal weapon at that time, and Ramirez's presence meant Texas could throw it easily running to either side.

Another area where Ramirez proved particularly adept was in helping Texas turn the momentum against longtime nemesis Oklahoma, with a 15-14 win in 1958 and a 19-12 victory in 1959, as the Longhorns went on to win eight straight in the series. He seemed to be forever throwing or catching touchdown passes against Bud Wilkinson's Sooners.

He finished his career in a 23-14 loss to national champion Syracuse in the Cotton Bowl, playing for a team ranked No. 4 in the nation.

"That was the last game I ever played, but there was almost one more," he says. "Coach Royal called me in and told me I had been picked to play in the Hula Bowl in Hawaii.

"He said Bud was one of the coaches and he made me his first pick, because he said he wasn't going to let me beat him again.

"There was another story back then where after one loss to us, he supposedly said, 'I got 10 white guys and one black guy who are the best money can buy, and I get beat by a left-handed Mexican.' I would have liked to have played for him, but I had a scheduling conflict."

The reason Ramirez turned down the Hawaii trip was that on January 30, 1960, he married his college sweetheart, Jo Marie Hill. It was a union that would last 28 years and produce seven children.

Having also quit his first love—baseball, Ramirez had laid his athletic career aside. By summertime, he was in the insurance business.

"I first went to work for Amicable Life, which became American Amicable and then something else, I forget what," he says. "Eventually, I had my own company. I lived in Austin from the time I got there in 1956 until 1976, when I went back to Hebbronville."

Retracing old footsteps.

"When I was growing up, my daddy [Tomas] was always involved in something," he says, "and us kids were always working at it, too. He owned a service station, where we worked, and a liquor store, and he also bought a ranch. When he died, he actually left us 250 acres, some cattle, and some rent houses.

"When I went back home, I kind of had a similar idea. Still selling insurance some, but basically an entrepreneur. I had a car wash, a barbeque place, an ice cream parlor, and bought a couple of ranches.

"Then in 1978 I ran for county judge and lost by 32 votes. I almost went into depression over it.

"But just then, Mobil called me and offered me a job as an engineer, and that kind of pulled me out of it. I was doing well, and they were real high on me, and I worked for them for five years. Eventually I accepted a job in their corporate offices in Houston."

By that time, Ramirez's youngest daughter, Jo Rikki, had been born. At about 18 months, she was diagnosed with leukemia.

"Nobody knows why," he says. "They don't know why that disease sometimes strikes little kids. It just does.

"So when I took the job in Houston and we went up there to look for a place to live, I'm driving along with my little daughter in the car, and all of a sudden there's this huge wreck right in front of us, and it just kind of freaked me out, and I said, 'I don't want to live here.'

"So I told them I had some personal problems and needed a leave of absence. I was too proud to admit I made a mistake, too ashamed to admit I'd screwed up. They said they didn't give leaves of absence, but then the president of their Southwest region, a friend of mine, called and told me to take whatever time I needed and come back whenever I wanted to."

At that point, the job was the least of Ramirez's concerns.

"When my daughter got sick, we took her to M.D. Anderson for treatment," he says. "She eventually went into remission after a bone marrow transplant. I was a donor.

"Then she went through radiation, then chemo for about a year. She was such a brave little girl. It just about killed me to see her go through that, but she never complained.

"When they started that treatment, they had me sign a release, because they said that with small children it affects the brain and reduces the mental capacity. There was no choice; I had to sign it.

"But everything turned out okay. She graduated from high school in the top five percent of her class, and now she's a math whiz with a college degree and a great job with an investment company in Austin. She's just terrific."

But when Ramirez was ready to go back to Mobil, he says, "The guy who had made me the promise had taken early retirement when the oil business went into a slump, and I never got the job back."

He was selling insurance again when his marriage began to fall apart in the mid-1980s.

"We separated in 1985, and then I moved back up to Austin to try and save it, but we just couldn't work it out," he says. "We divorced in January of 1988. It's the greatest regret of my life. She's a beautiful lady."

The couple's seven children—Teresa, Eric, Celeste, Alan, Rene (Mario), Carlos, and Jo Rikki—all live near their mother in the Austin area. Aside from Jo Rikki, two are attorneys, one is an accountant, one is a teacher, one is a CPA, and one does computer work for a communications company.

Having reached a point where "I couldn't have sold a hamburger to a hungry guy," Ramirez got out of the insurance business and looked for something new. A friend, Austin attorney Wally Scott, helped him find it.

"Through his contacts, I got a job with the state that I've held ever since," he says. "Originally I was doing a lot of surveying all around the state. But I was looking to settle down again and so they said, 'Can you do appraisals?' So that's what I've been doing the last several years. I work for the General Land Office.

"It's mostly state-owned properties such as warehouses and other buildings, but we've also done several elements of the prison system."

He and his second wife, Becky (Laura Rebecca)—who he met in Monterrey, Mexico—have been married 16 years and have two children: Adrian, 14, and Emmanuel, 13.

"Her aunt was a longtime friend of mine in Austin," he says. "I met her on a visit down there, and then she came up here, and things just worked out.

"Now I live in McAllen, and my boss sends me my assignments from Austin, and it's a good job.

"I still have a small place in Hebbronville. My mother, [Dora], is 87 and still going strong, and my brothers are over there. Hector is a justice of the peace, and Tomas is still teaching. My other brother, Greg, really made the best career move.

"He's a retired teacher, bringing in about $10,000 to $12,000 per month, because his wife inherited some property with gas wells on it."

Where Have You Gone?

JAMES SAXTON

When James Saxton left Austin for a business trip to Dallas in late October 1994, he was, at 54, a former athlete in excellent condition who had never had a serious medical problem in his life.

When he returned a few days later, he knew something was terribly wrong.

"I had started feeling really strange," he says, "and in fact I just barely made it back home. I told Carol Ann, my wife, 'I need to go to the hospital.'"

When he arrived at the emergency room, Saxton's condition was diagnosed as viral encephalitis, and he was given drugs to treat it.

Then he went into a coma.

When he came out of it, Saxton was returned to a world dramatically different from the one he had left. But at least he was alive.

"I was in a coma for many days, weeks," he says. "I almost died—many people do in that situation. But they gave me a new drug for it, and I think that saved my life. I was just lucky the people in the emergency room knew what was going on."

He eventually returned to the Guaranty Bank in Austin, but the job holds a few new challenges. His short-term memory is faulty, his hearing and speech patterns were affected, and he can't remember numbers.

"What happened to me was, I caught a virus, just like a lot of people do," he says. "This one attacks the right side of the brain. Nobody knows why one person catches it and another doesn't. There's no rhyme or reason to it.

"It just happened all of a sudden. I'm sure I must have had some sensation of feeling sluggish or something, but I really don't remember.

"I'm lucky I survived, because many people don't. And there's not really a whole lot of treatment for the damaged part of the brain.

"I went through therapy for my memory. And I was having trouble talking, so they did therapy on me for that. There's been no difference physically—I still work out and stay in shape. But my speech has changed a lot.

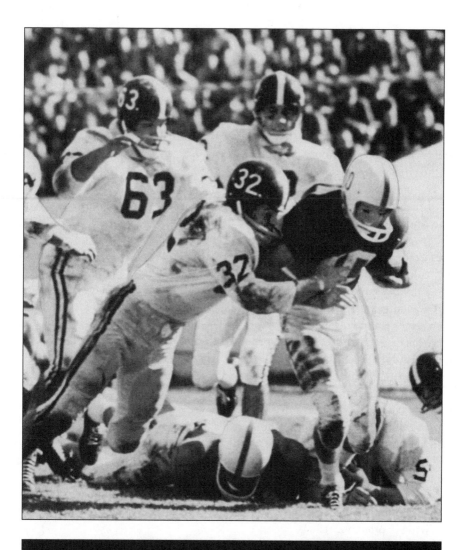

JAMES SAXTON
Hgt: 5-11 • Wgt: 164 • Hometown: Palestine

Years played: 1959-1961
Position: Halfback
Highlights: 1961: All-SWC, Consensus All-American;
finished third in Heisman Trophy voting; led SWC in rushing
with 846 yards and 7.9 average

"I'd say my condition has improved, but it still presents a problem with short-term memory. It continues to affect me, trying to remember things, remember people, remember numbers.

"It also affected my hearing to the extent that I would have a problem in business meetings—sometimes I couldn't hear a thing in the whole meeting. So now I wear a hearing aid."

Saxton smiles and adds, "The blessing about the whole thing was that it left me with my long-term memory and information, so I can remember and think about all the good things in my life."

Foremost among these is Carol Ann, his high school sweetheart.

"I had my first date with her," he says, "back when we were going to school in Palestine. She's been my lifelong sweetheart.

"In a way, we actually got separated when we graduated from high school, because I went to Texas and she went to SMU. But we stayed in touch every day with a letter or phone call.

"I also played extra hard when we played SMU, which is probably why I always had a good game against them. We got married the year I graduated [1962], and she's been with me through everything."

A lot of good things also happened to Saxton while he was playing at Texas (1959-1961), particularly in his senior year, when he finished third in the voting for the Heisman Trophy. He ended the season a consensus All-American with 846 yards rushing at 7.9 per carry and nine touchdowns. He actually played about half of each game, because the Longhorns usually won so easily.

Texas won the Cotton Bowl, but finished 10-1 because of a 6-0 loss to TCU in which Saxton was knocked out of the game in the first half.

"I actually got kicked in the head," he says. "The only good thing about that game was that I slept through it."

As for the other games, Saxton attributes his success to his teammates, including Jack Collins, the other halfback, who became a wingback when Texas switched to the Wing-T offense in 1961.

"I take my hat off to Jack," he says. "He went downfield and threw the key block on every long run I made. I appreciate what he did, because Jack really took a lot and did the best he could all the time. He was All-Conference as a sophomore and then moved to wingback and blocked for me. He had as much talent as anyone and could have been in my shoes if they hadn't changed the offense.

"Also, the main thing about that Texas team is we had the best linemen. Don Talbert and Ed Padgett and the others opened huge holes, and I just ran through them."

In 1996, he was inducted into the National Football Foundation Hall of Fame.

That would have seemed a remote possibility when Saxton was growing up in Palestine in the 1950s.

"My dad was an alcoholic," he says. "He and my mother divorced when I was two, and I never saw him again. But I had a grandfather who taught me to hunt and fish and things like that.

"My mom [Rachel] worked. My aunt owned a laundry/dry cleaning operation, and Mom was the general manager.

"But it burned down, and after that she got various other jobs to take care of me and my sister. She worked hard and did everything possible to get me into the right places. We didn't want for very much because she made us understand that we were fortunate for what we had.

"She later remarried, but the second guy was also an alcoholic, and it

James Saxton (*Photo courtesy of the Saxton family*)

was as bad as the first marriage. But she worked hard to make sure my sister, Martha, and I were raised properly."

One thing Saxton remembers about his youth is that his sister could outrun him. She was one of the few people in the state of Texas who could make that claim.

When Saxton was a senior at Texas, he still weighed only 164 pounds, but there wasn't a slow ounce in there anywhere. They were calling him "Rabbit" long before he left Palestine.

"Most of the Southwest Conference schools recruited me," he says, "but I committed to Texas on my first trip.

"But I had an aunt who was a friend of [Rice coach] Jess Neely's wife, and they started working on me through her. I remember going down there, and Neely took me to the upper deck of that huge stadium and waved his hand and said, 'This is yours if you want it.'

"I called Coach Royal to tell him I was uncommitted, and he said, 'My God, don't do that!' He said, 'I'm coming over there to Palestine, and I don't want to see your mother, aunt, sister, or any woman. You just come out and sit in the car with me, and we'll talk.'

"So I did, and by the time we were through, I was an Orange-blood."

It turned out to be a mutually beneficial decision.

"Coach Royal, he was really my idol, I guess you could say," Saxton says. "Coming from a one-parent family, being raised by my mother, he gave me a father image I had never had before. He got me started in the right direction."

Momentarily, however, Saxton felt Royal was pushing him in the wrong direction.

"Originally, he brought me in as a quarterback," Saxton says, laughing. "He said he wanted a running quarterback. I didn't know the difference between that and any other kind of quarterback, and I had never played the position except to fill in when our starter got hurt in high school. He put in some run-pass option plays for me, but he would say, 'Now James, don't you throw the ball, just run it.'

"Finally one day he was showing me how to set up under center and call the cadence. But when I started calling the cadence, I had such a high-pitched voice I sounded like a little kid, and he said, 'Oh, we've got a lot of work to do.'"

Eventually, Royal decided that Saxton would be more useful in a running back slot, and an All-America halfback was born.

After Saxton left Texas, life in the NFL beckoned, but not for long.

"I was drafted by the Dallas Texans," he says, "so I signed for a $5,000 bonus and a $20,000 salary and played there in 1962. The money was good, but the rest of it wasn't.

"It was no fun, not what I associated the game with. The players were a lot different, and the atmosphere was nothing like college. Plus I still weighed about 170, and I didn't play much.

"We beat Houston in the longest game in history [two full overtimes] to win the AFL championship. But the next year they moved to Kansas City and became the Chiefs, and I wasn't enjoying it anyway, so I decided to just stay in Texas and try to get a job.

"I went to work on an executive training program for the First National Bank in Dallas and worked there for seven years. Then one of our chief officers had a chance to go to Austin, and he invited me to come with him.

"So I did and eventually moved over to Guaranty Bank, and I've been here ever since. When I was sick, the bank was very helpful in working with me and helping me with the recovery. The people here have been wonderful."

Deciding to go to Texas long ago, he says, was one of the best decisions of his life.

"It gave me a good education and an opportunity to meet a lot of people," he says. "There have always been a lot of people who at least knew my name, and it has led to business opportunities.

"I've had some ups and downs, but I'm thoroughly convinced that if I hadn't achieved what I did in football, I might not have achieved what I have since."

The Saxtons have three children: Jimmy, who played football at UT in the early 1990s and is now a State Farm agent in Burnet; Cathy, who runs a summer camp that includes bungee jumps and mountain climbing in Vail, Colorado, with her husband; and Shelley, whose husband is the golf pro at the Four Seasons in Dallas.

And each other.

"Carol Ann gives a lot of her time to charitable organizations," he says. "And she's a good caretaker. She's nursed me through a lot of problems."

Where Have You Gone?

JAMES STREET

L ong ago, the operable phrase for a particularly challenging venture was coined
by Texas assistant coach Mike Campbell.

"Taking your team into Fayetteville," he said, "is like parachuting into Russia."

It certainly seemed at least that perilous on December 6, 1969, when two
unbeaten teams battled for national supremacy in front of a national viewing audi-
ence and a packed house at Razorback Stadium that included the Rev. Billy Graham
and President Richard M. Nixon.

In the event, the Longhorns were fortunately led by the perfect individual to
yank the ripcord and yell, "Geronimo!" on his way into battle:

Quarterback James Street, the man they called "Slick."

Then again, a mere parachute drop into impending disaster seems a bit tame.
This one looked more like a remake of *The Iliad*, with the Razorbacks, fighting in
their home fortress, portraying the valiant, doomed Trojans, and the Longhorns—
led by their own wily Odysseus—assuming the guise of the invading Greeks. An
epic clash for the favor of the gods.

In the end, the Longhorns won that favor—in the polls and with the endorse-
ment of the president—and were proclaimed national champions. They won it
largely with a brilliant gamble called Right 53 Veer Pass that was fully worthy of
your best Trojan Horse ruse.

It was a call for which Darrell Royal was eternally proclaimed a coaching
genius—not that there was any lack of such consideration previously—and a play
that stamped Street as the quintessential River Boat Gambler: The man who would
never lose.

An all-star pitcher on three College World Series teams and the undefeated (20-0)
quarterback who launched the Wishbone era at Texas, Street now has his own company—The James Street Group—and a large, busy family in Austin.

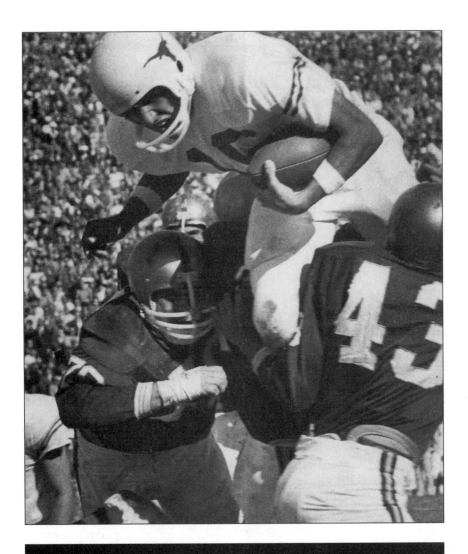

JAMES STREET
Hgt: 5-11 • Wgt: 175 • Hometown: Longview

Years played: 1968-1969
Position: Quarterback
Highlights: 1969: All-SWC; led Texas to victories over Arkansas in The Great Shootout and Notre Dame in the Cotton Bowl to clinch a national championship; finished with 20-0 record as starting quarterback; 1968-1970: All-SWC pitcher on three College World Series teams; 1969-1970: Second-team All-American

He also has the vague feeling that he may have been involved in the longest game in history, saying, "It amazes me that people still talk about it and think about it and rehash it after 35 years."

He was particularly amazed last year when a reunion was organized—by the Arkansas players.

"That really impressed me," he says, "because I know that for a lot of those people up there, it has never been over. For many in that state, it was the most bitter disappointment in their lives, and they have never forgotten it. Especially the way it happened, it had to be a heartbreaking loss.

"But if you look at all the other things surrounding it—the climax of the 100th year of college football, the president being there, No. 1 matched up against No. 2— it does take on a different aura. Plus, 1969 seemed like a year when so many strange things happened.

"Then you have the No. 1 team falling behind and coming back to win in the end. If you had been doing a movie script, that's exactly the way you would write it. So it comes down as a famous game—and I guess all those guys from Arkansas realized that they were a part of history."

Indeed, 1969 was a little strange. It was the year of Woodstock—and also, the week of the game, a Rolling Stones concert in California near the Altamont Freeway, in which a fan was stabbed to death by a member of the Hell's Angels, who were acting as security police. Also the week of the game, Charles Manson was formally charged in the Sharon Tate murders.

On the flip side, ABC had taken the advice of Beano Cook and arranged to move the Texas–Arkansas game—normally played in October—to the end of the season in hopes of a possible showdown for the national title. A decision, Royal later said, that made the network "look smarter than a tree full of owls."

Royal himself was not exactly afflicted with an idle mind, Street recalls.

"One thing I'll never forget," he says, "is him sitting there with me on the bus showing me the play we would call if we needed a two-point conversion. He was having a little trouble keeping my attention, because frankly I thought we would win easily enough that we wouldn't need one. But he made sure I knew the play."

At the end of the third quarter, with Arkansas leading 14-0 and dominating the game with its defense, it appeared that Street was right: Texas probably would not need a two-point conversion.

But on the first play of the fourth quarter, Street turned a busted play into a 42-yard touchdown run, and it was suddenly a new game. Street then ran the counter option play Royal had instructed him to use, and it was 14-8.

"He had learned that from a game he lost to Arkansas 14-13 in 1964, when a two-point conversion attempt failed late in the game," Street says. "This time he was going to give himself an extra chance at it if it came down to that and at least get a tie. But now we were in a position to win."

Not for long, it seemed. Arkansas swept back downfield, inside the Texas 10-yard line with a chance for at least a possible game-clinching field goal. But first, the

Razorbacks went for the touchdown, and Danny Lester intercepted Bill Montgomery's pass in the end zone and ran it back out to the 20, setting up the winning drive.

When the climactic moment came, with the Longhorns facing fourth and three at their 43 and time growing short, Street learned another lesson from the coach he considers to be a flat-out genius.

"I was over on the sideline talking with Coach Royal and coach [Emory] Bellard, who was up in the booth," he says. "Coach Bellard and I both wanted to run the counter option to pick up the first down. But while we were discussing it, Coach Royal pulled off the headset and said it: 'Right 53 Veer Pass.'

"This was a deep pass with only one receiver—the tight end, Randy Peschel—going out in the pattern. It was the most improbable call you could make in that situation, which, of course, is why Royal called it. But as soon as he said it, Mike Campbell started yelling for the defense to get ready, because he didn't think it would work.

"I started back to the huddle—and then I came back to Coach Royal and I said, 'Are you sure?' And he said, 'Damn right, I'm sure.'

"So I went back out to the huddle and said, 'Boys, you ain't gonna believe this....'"

A careful chap, Street made a point of looking straight at split end Cotton Speyrer and saying, "Peschel, don't look at me!" while calling the play, because he believed the Razorbacks had been trying to look into the Texas huddle in an attempt to identify who would get the ball on the next play. He also told Peschel to doubleback for a shorter pass if he couldn't get open deep.

But Peschel ran the route as planned, and Street hit him with a 44-yard bomb that swung the momentum in favor of the Longhorns.

"As soon as I threw the ball," Street says, "I got hit by Terry Don Phillips, who had been a teammate of mine in high school at Longview. I was lying down on the ground, trying to see what happened, and finally I spotted Peschel down on the ground with the ball after the catch.

"So I picked Terry Don up and said, 'Come on, Bubba, we're way down yonder.'"

With a first down at the 13, the Longhorns ran Ted Koy for 11, with a key block from Jim Bertelsen, who then ran the final two yards for the touchdown that—with a game-clinching interception by Tom Campbell moments later—gave Texas a 15-14 victory. They soon received President Nixon's blessing as national champions and finished that way in the polls.

"On Koy's run, Bertelsen actually missed his first block but went on to hit the linebacker, which opened up the lane," Street says. "From that, the coaches learned that it was what we should have been doing all day. They made that adjustment for the Arkansas game the next year and won 42-7."

If the Longhorns had won this one 42-7, no one would have remembered it 35 years later.

For the presidentially anointed champs, one chore remained: beat Notre Dame. This was accomplished when Street drove the Longhorns 76 yards on their final possession for the winning touchdown in a 21-17 battle in the Cotton Bowl.

The key play came with Texas facing fourth and two at the Irish 10-yard line. Street rolled left and threw a low wobbly pass toward Speyrer, who made a diving catch at the two-yard line. Two plays later, Billy Dale scored from the one.

"After the game," Street says, "the reporters were asking me about that pass, and I said, 'Well, I could tell by the way they were covering Cotton that the best place to throw it was low and behind him,' and that's actually the way it was written in the stories."

There also seems to have been some lingering doubt about the exact sequence leading to the demise of the Fighting Irish.

"It's amazing," Street says, "how many times over the years I've been at some gathering or party where someone has told me they'll never forget me throwing the touchdown pass to Cotton that beat Notre Dame.

"I used to point out that the pass to Cotton was for a first down, and that Billy Dale scored the touchdown a couple of plays later. But I've had people call me a liar and tell me I don't know what I'm talking about, and start cussing me, telling me they were there and they saw it.

"So I just don't argue with them anymore."

As for Right 53 Veer Pass, he says, it was pure Darrell Royal.

"He did stuff like that for 20 years in showdown games," Street says. "He's like a poker player who will play every hand according to the percentages until the game gets down to what I call scoot 'em. Then with everything on the line, he'll do something totally different from what you expect him to do."

For Street, a promising baseball career at UT included a 29-8 career record and two no-hitters but ended with an arm injury in the College World Series. He returned to Austin and went into business and has headed his own company for the last 14 years.

That isn't the end of the baseball story, however.

Street and his wife, Janie, have four sons—Huston, 21, twins Jordan and Justin, 18, and Hanson, 17. The three youngest are still in school. Huston, now in his second season of pro ball, has moved into the closer role for the Oakland Athletics.

An All-America closer at Texas, he impressed fans and scouts alike with good stuff, a sweeping sidearm delivery, and a coolness under pressure that seemed to suggest a family influence.

"I learned a lot from my dad," Huston says. "I remember him saying that he always tried to do his best on every play—whether the game was on the line or not—and that if you can learn that approach you'll probably come through okay. And that's the way I pitch.

"The first time I ever pitched in the College World Series, he took me aside the night before and said, 'I know what you're going to do; I've been there. You're going to look up and see 20,000 people, and your heart will start pounding, and you'll go out there thinking you have to do more. And you'll end up trying to do too much. Remember it's the same game, just a different ballpark.' That really helped me a lot.

"Actually, I think he's helped prepare all of us to deal with pressure. We've always been very competitive among ourselves, and if he was involved, he never just let us win—whether it was Horse or ping pong or pitching pennies or what. He never got mad at us for not doing well. He always said just do your best and don't make excuses."

Credit ol' dad with an assist.

"Whenever we did something like that," Street says, "I never wanted to just roll over and let them win, because I think you're sending the wrong message. In real life, people aren't going to roll over and let you win, and I think kids need to learn that at an early age. If you win, you earn it."

Although all of his kids are athletic, Street says he never pushed anyone in that direction, although he has been ready with helpful advice. This also includes his oldest son, Ryan, from a previous marriage.

"He's 30 now, and he has become a very successful architect. He has a lot of talent, and he's good friends with Lance Armstrong and does a lot of stuff for him.

"At one time, he was going to go off and play football at Texas Tech, but they wouldn't give him a scholarship. So he was going to walk on.

"I told him, 'Look, I'm going to love you whether you play football or not. I got to see you play in high school and that was great, but now you need to think longer term. Everything in life is a time commitment. Think about what you want to do.'

"I said, 'Remember the time in high school when we were out in West Texas in a hospital wrapping a sheet around your arm so they could pop your shoulder back in place? Well, in this league you want to play in now, they're a lot bigger and a lot faster. They're going to knock that shoulder out again. They're going to knock you into next week. It's not a good use of your time, because you're not going to play pro ball.'

"I said, 'Go to college, get involved, meet everyone, get to know people. Get involved in management, get on committees, learn where the money goes. Think about what you want to be. If you come out with a degree and an idea what you want to do, you'll be 10 years ahead of your daddy. Because I had no clue, and I was the quarterback on a national champion.'

"Well, he skipped football, and he's done such a great job with his life that when we had a conversation recently, I congratulated him on that and added that I was kind of proud myself for giving him that advice.

"So he just smiled and said, 'Dad, back then I really thought you were an old man who didn't know what he was talking about, and I fully intended to walk on and play football at Tech. But when I got there, I had a roommate who was two inches taller and about 30 to 40 pounds heavier than I was, and he had gone out for football the year before. He got knocked about and beat up pretty bad and was hurt all the time, and he told me, "If you try to go out for football, you're crazy. All you'll ever be out there is one of the dummies who never plays." So that's why I quit thinking about football. It had nothing to do with that speech you gave me.'"

Street laughs and says he'll still be available with helpful advice in the future.

And as for that moment long ago, when the Texas players emerged from a desperate battle with something akin to the status of immortals—

"Huston once had four saves in the College World Series," he says, "and I had a game up in Fayetteville that people are still asking me about 35 years later. You have to get lucky for that to happen and have a lot of other people around you making it happen.

"A quarterback gets a lot of credit—but I had nothing to do with Danny Lester intercepting that pass and running it out of the end zone or Randy Peschel leaping up and making that great catch or Tom Campbell intercepting that pass at the end.

"Championships are won—as a team."

Where Have You Gone?

BEN TOMPKINS

One day as a sage old gent of about 30, Ben Tompkins finally took a cold, clear look at where he was headed down the road of life—and immediately hung a hard right.

At that point, he had completed a successful athletic career at the University of Texas, two years in the Army, and six seasons of professional baseball. He had a growing family and what suddenly seemed like shrinking options.

"I began to look my life over, and realized that up to that point, I had always felt that nothing really mattered except a ball of some sort," he says. "I thought maybe I ought to take a different view of things.

"I had children getting ready to start school, and I felt I needed to get something different going. At some point, I had become interested in law, and that became my focus.

"I can't say I was disappointed over the end of my baseball career—I thoroughly enjoyed the time I spent playing ball—but I knew it was time to move on to something else."

So Tompkins, a 1948 graduate of Fort Worth's Poly High School, returned home to the East Side and began plotting a law career.

"I took courses at Texas Wesleyan a couple of summers, went to work at LTV [in Dallas], and in 1962 enrolled in law school at SMU and began commuting," he says. "I did that for three years."

Degree in hand, Tompkins went to work as a prosecutor in the district attorney's office in Fort Worth and stayed three years. For the next several years he did criminal defense work, first with a partner and then solo, with his own firm.

"I did that until 1982 when I went into the insurance defense business in Dallas with a firm that became known as Reynolds and Tompkins," he says. "We represented Travelers as a major client.

BEN TOMPKINS
Hgt: 6-0 • Wgt: 175 • Hometown: Fort Worth

Year played: 1950
Position: Quarterback
Highlights: 1950: Starting quarterback on a team ranked No. 3
in the nation; 1949-1950: Infielder on two
College World Series championship teams

"I left after three years to form a defense office in Texas for Fireman's Fund, but they never developed the volume they expected, so I left after three years and was hired to reorganize the defense office for the AIG, which was always in chaos."

Deciding to "move over to the plaintiff's side," he joined Bailey, Galyen, and Gold in Fort Worth to form a personal injury office and has been with the firm ever since.

Most of the time this was going on, however, Tompkins also had an alternate occupation.

In 1953, out of the Army and waiting for spring training, Tompkins officiated a few junior high football games to pass the time and make some extra money. Nearly 40 years later—after 20 seasons in the NFL—he officiated his last game.

"I loved officiating," he says. "It was a lot of fun. I was doing college games in the 1960s and finally I wound up for two years doing games in the Missouri Valley Conference—and then I got jumped up to the NFL.

"The explanation for that is that in the late 1960s, the pass-oriented offenses they ran in the MVC were closer to the pro game than the run-oriented attacks you saw in the Southwest Conference. So the MVC officials were the ones being promoted, and I went to the NFL in 1971."

He stayed for two decades, working two Super Bowls and dozens of playoff games and key matchups, including a game in the snow in Buffalo when O.J. Simpson set a new rushing record.

"You always hear about pressure in big games," he says. "Actually, the bigger the game, the easier it was. In those situations you had two good, well-coached teams who knew what they were doing and were careful not to hurt their cause with stupid mistakes. I enjoyed that aspect, and it was quite challenging.

"Usually it went very smoothly. It was when you had losing teams with bad attitudes and nothing to play for that you had trouble.

"I also got great cooperation all those years from the people in the court system here. I could always go in and tell the judge, 'I've got a game in Seattle,' or 'I've got a Monday night game,' and he would reschedule the court appearance and let me go. They usually wanted to sit down and talk about the game or the players with me anyway.

"I know it's hard to believe, but my favorite coach was Norm Van Brocklin. He was vitriolic and didn't get along with a lot of people, but he and I got along very well. He was smart and clever, and he never turned anyone in to the league office. If he had a problem, he told you about it right then and there, and that's where it stayed.

"I also liked Don Shula. He was a great coach, and I respected him. I got into a run-in with him once, and the next Miami game I did, he gave me the cold shoulder—a little one-upmanship. But the next one was a playoff game with a lot on the line, and when I walked in the locker room, he hit me with a big smile and said, 'Ben, how are you? Welcome to Miami.'

"When I did Oakland games, I used to talk to Marcus Allen a lot, and when there was a timeout, I would go over to the sideline and talk to Jim Garner, who was usually standing there. I don't know why he was a Raiders fan, but he was."

After 20 NFL years, Tompkins's decision to retire was formed before a game in Cleveland, when he was walking under the stadium with a crew member.

"He was all keyed up and suddenly just tossed his cookies," Tompkins says. "And he asked me if I got excited before the games. Later, I thought about it and realized there wasn't that much excitement anymore—maybe I'd been doing this too long, and it was time to get out. So I did."

At UT, Tompkins had a dual career, and 1950 was a very good year. In the spring, he played on a baseball team that won the national championship under Bibb Falk, and in the fall he quarterbacked a team that went 9-1 with a 14-13 loss to Oklahoma, the national champion.

"We should have won that game," he says. "At the end of the first half, we were down on their goal line, and there was some controversy about whether we scored or not, but we wound up with nothing. Then late in the game we dropped a snap on a punt, and they recovered and had a short drive for the winning touchdown.

"At midseason, we had a showdown game with SMU, which was led by Kyle Rote and was ranked No. 1 and being written up in *Life* magazine. We won that one 23-20 and went on to face Tennessee in the Cotton Bowl. I think we really wanted to play OU again, and we didn't play well and lost 20-14."

After that, Tompkins weighed his options: return to Texas for his senior year or take a $25,000 signing bonus from the Phillies. He took the bonus, but two days later he got his draft notice and spent the next two years in the service, mostly playing football.

In 1953, he began his professional baseball career with an MVP year at Terre Haute, where he hit .318. He spent the next five years at the Triple-A level, two at Syracuse and three at Miami, once playing in the Little World Series.

"When they moved the Triple-A club to Miami, we got a little surprise on opening night," Tompkins says. "About the second or third inning, a helicopter lands on the field and out steps Satchel Paige.

"He was with us for the next few years. He was about 54 or 55 then, but he could still throw as hard as anyone in the league if the weather was warm. If the weather was cold, you might not see him at all.

"I don't think he ever knew anybody's name—he called me 'Second Base'—but it was great being around him and listening to his stories."

Looking over his life, Tompkins says there is one thing he would change if he could.

"I had a great educational opportunity at Texas, which I didn't take advantage of," he says. "I'd say that was probably immaturity.

"I had a terrible attitude as a kid. I didn't want to go to class too early, didn't care about grades, had the attitude of 'Just get me by and provide help if I need it.'

"Later, I decided to make some changes in my life, and I did, and I'm proud of that. I'm also proud of the law career I've had, because in the beginning people told me I couldn't do it alone, but I did.

"From a selfish standpoint, practicing law is like playing baseball or football to me. There's the competition, the winners and losers, you've got to figure out, 'What am I going to do with this situation?' You've got to change strategies at midstream much of the time, and I like that."

Tompkins and his wife, Shirley, have been married for 36 years and have four children: Becky, a housewife in Colleyville; Bob, who works in computer software in San Diego; Sandra, who lives in Santa Cruz and works in computers; and Luanne, a biologist living in Saginaw.

And at 75, Tompkins, who looks 15 years younger, says he has no plans to retire.

"I'm doing what I really enjoy doing," he says. "My health is good. People normally guess my age at being considerably younger, and that's the way I feel. People ask me if I'm still working, and I say, 'Yeah, I'm working, why not?'

"I'll retire when I go out in a box."

Where Have You Gone?

BYRON TOWNSEND

A ssessing his time spent on the planet to this point, at age 75 Byron Townsend is inclined toward the modest appraisal.

"I guess you'd say it's been a pretty dull life," he says.

In terms of accuracy, this one would rank right up there with a statement from the pope saying he thinks Christianity is overrated.

"Santone" Townsend's life has certainly had its share of off-road accidents—along with some notable highlights—but it ain't ever been dull.

"Actually, it's been pretty good so far," he says, on further reflection.

A lot of that has to do with his marrying Ramona 35 years ago. But there have been other memorable moments as well.

As a brief review, Townsend first achieved prominence as a star fullback on a legendary West Texas high school team that won a state championship and 26 straight games before running afoul of the evil genius of a college coach in Dallas.

Moving on to the University of Texas, he became one of the most acclaimed backs in the nation as a junior—on a team that nearly won a national championship—despite the gnawing feeling that he was playing the wrong position in the wrong offense, maybe for the wrong coach.

As a senior, he was a prime All-America candidate until a slight mishap occurred: He nearly had his leg ripped off.

Moving on, he was well into a comeback with the Los Angeles Rams when Uncle Sam called, as was frequently the case during the Korean War era.

Back from the service and cut by the Rams, he moved to Canada and was having a good year in Winnipeg when he was examined for a neck injury—at which point the doctor informed him that nobody else with a spine that looked like his was stupid enough to try playing professional football.

Returning to Odessa, where he played high school ball, he worked for a trucking firm and then, he says, "followed the uranium mining boom to Arizona," where nothing much happened except for the time the local sheriff asked for his help in

Years played: 1949-1951
Position: Fullback
Highlights: 1950: All-SWC; rushed for 105 yards against Tennessee in the
Cotton Bowl; ranks 15th on all-time UT rushing list with 1,783 yards

removing the bloody corpse of a murder victim from a pond, which also ended the investigation into the matter.

Back in Odessa, he began doing blueprints on construction sites, until he and some pals decided to spend a couple of relaxing weeks in Alaska on vacation. He stayed 25 years, working for an oil company (UNICAL). He did make one phone call back to Odessa and talked Ramona into moving to Alaska to get married.

They adopted two kids: "a gorgeous little girl"—Tracey Amber, now 31, and a son, Mickey ("named after Mickey Mantle"), now 27.

After Townsend retired from the oil company, he and Ramona moved back to Texas—first to Fredericksburg and later to Kerrville. Over the 2004 Christmas holidays, they traveled to Virginia to visit two new additions to the family—Tracey Amber's twin daughters, born the day after Christmas.

In other respects, recent events have been less pleasant. Townsend had a heart attack in 2002, and now wears a pacemaker. Around the same time, a business deal the couple had invested in heavily went sour, and he says, "The last couple of years have not been good."

Finally, a doctor recently told him "that I have the beginnings of Alzheimer's disease," he says. "So, I guess I'm sort of hoping that either he's wrong—or they come up with something pretty quick."

In all, a rather eventful life. And it's still going.

"My dad worked for Humble Oil Co.," he says, "and we moved around some. I was born in Crane, but before I was five we moved to Lytle, about 18 miles south of San Antonio. When I was 12, he got transferred to Odessa, and that's where I started playing football."

As a junior in 1946, Townsend played on a team that for many years afterward was still considered one of the best ever assembled. In addition to Townsend, the backfield included Hayden Fry, Pug Gabrel, and Sonny Holderman, all of whom went on to distinguished careers after high school.

The Bronchos rolled to a 14-0 record and a state title, and the championship game against San Antonio Jefferson was a classic—pitting Townsend in a duel with future SMU star Kyle Rote in front of a crowd of 38,000 in Austin. Both players scored once and threw a touchdown pass, but Odessa came up with an extra score and won 21-14.

"That was the first time Kyle and I did battle, but it would happen several times over the years," Townsend says. "We really had a great team that year—in fact, every guy on it except one went to college on a scholarship, and that was pretty unusual."

The following year, the Bronchos were sitting on 12-0 when they faced Highland Park in the semifinals, and Townsend figures that, "We must have been favored by about 60 points."

But one of the Highland Park players was H.N. (Rusty) Russell Jr., whose father had coached Fort Worth Masonic Home's legendary "Mighty Mites" in the 1930s before moving to Highland Park during the war, where he coached Doak Walker and Bobby Layne.

He was now Matty Bell's chief assistant at SMU and was, in fact, the architect of the Mustangs' famed wide-open offense. But he wasn't bad at defense, either.

"We thought we'd roll over them, but every play we ran, they knew what we were going to do before we ran it," Townsend says. "They stopped us cold all day and beat us 18-6. We found out later that Rusty Sr. had gone over that week and helped them prepare for us. He must have had a film or something, because he did a helluva job.

"It's funny, you'd think that would be something you'd forget about soon enough, but I never have. That loss to Highland Park hurt me more than any other that I was involved in, and to this day I still think about it. I've never put it out of my mind, and even now, I probably remember it about once a week."

But there were a couple at Texas that left their mark.

The 1950 Longhorns went 9-1 and finished the regular season as the third-ranked team in the nation. The only defeat was a 14-13 loss to the team that ended the season ranked No. 1—Oklahoma.

"We should have won that game," Townsend says. "We lost it on two weird plays, and the first one was just a really bad, bad call by the official. It happened right before the half when we were on their three, and I got the ball and went in and scored. I know that because I looked down and saw the goal line beneath me, and I had crossed it.

"But then the stack got shoved back, and someone knocked the ball out of my hands and an OU player fell on it, and the next thing I know the ref was hollering, 'First down, Oklahoma!' Bad call.

"We were still ahead late in the game, when our punter dropped the snap when he was trying to flip the ball over, and they recovered and got an easy touchdown three plays later and won it by kicking the extra point."

Three weeks later the Longhorns faced SMU in the final battle between Townsend and Rote. The Mustangs, undefeated with a victory over Ohio State, were at that point ranked No. 1 in the nation, but Texas pulled off a 23-20 upset and went unbeaten the rest of the way.

"The thing I remember about that game," Townsend says, "is that one of the touchdowns I scored, I stepped right on Bud McFadin's back and dove into the end zone. When we got to the sidelines, he pulled up his jersey and there were cleat marks on his back, and he said, 'It's a good thing you scored a touchdown, you silly son-of-a-bitch!'"

In the Cotton Bowl, the Longhorns played a strangely uninspired game and eventually lost 20-14 to Tennessee. It was Blair Cherry's last game, but Townsend is not inclined toward sentimentality.

"By that time, I was not happy with the offense we ran or my role in it," he says. "To be honest, I'd have to say I wish I had played for another coach.

"Blair Cherry believed in hard-nosed football—run straight ahead as hard as you can. Every play in our offense was designed to gain four to five yards. None of them were designed for you to break a long run, and you were not allowed to cut back or change directions.

"Even though I played fullback in high school, I broke a lot of long runs and I was used to cutting back, trying to make tacklers miss, and gain as much yardage and score as often as possible. I did not understand Cherry's offense.

"But he actually called me in when I was ready to start playing and he said, 'I know how you run, and that's fine. But it's not the way we do it here. You run hard straight ahead, or you don't play. In the season opener, I cut back out of pure instinct and ran about 60 yards, and he yanked me out of the game. So when Ed Price became the coach in 1951, I was elated."

Having rushed for nearly 1,000 yards the previous year, he was also touted as a leading All-America candidate. But the elation and expectation lasted only a few games. On the opening kickoff against SMU, Townsend suffered an injury that gave new meaning to the term *out for the season.*

"I was running upfield with the ball with a blocker in front of me, but he missed the tackler," he says. "The guy hit me full speed in the thigh, right above the knee. One of my feet was planted in the turf and the other leg went straight up in the air. After two days, my whole leg was black, from the hip to the ankle.

"What had happened was, the muscle was basically torn in half and torn off the bone. I was on crutches for six weeks, and even after that, sometimes I would be just walking down the street and suddenly my leg would buckle and I would fall down. It took months for the muscle to grow back, and I still have a knot in my leg to this day.

"It was a devastating injury."

So ended Townsend's career at Texas—but he still ranks 15th on the school's all-time rushing list with 1,783 yards (and 22 touchdowns).

"I was drafted by the Rams, and I was healed enough to go to camp with them, and I was holding my own pretty well," he says. "Then after we played the College All-Stars in Chicago, one of the coaches came around and told me, 'You got a letter, and it's from Uncle Sam.'

"When I got out of the Army, I went back to the Rams, but I was out of shape and got cut. Then I got a call from the Winnipeg franchise up in the Canadian League, and they said they wanted to talk to me.

"I went up and talked to them, and wound up signing a contract for a hell of a lot more money than the Rams were paying. So I played for them in 1955 and had a really good year, and we went into the last game needing to win to play in the Grey Cup.

"But I had injured my neck, so I went to get it checked with a doctor. I had had neck problems all my life—sometimes I could just turn the wrong way shaving and get a crick in my neck. So I wasn't worried about it.

"But after they looked at the X-rays, the doctor came out and said, 'Townsend, your football days are over.' He told me that the shape my spine was in, I could get jarred real hard and be paralyzed from the neck down."

So Townsend quit football and devoted himself to less risky pursuits. Mostly.

Byron, Ramona, Mickey, and Tracey Amber Townsend (*Photo courtesy of the Townsend family*)

He worked for a trucking company for a while and then headed to Arizona to try his hand at mining uranium. It wasn't necessarily enriching, but it wasn't dull.

"I wound up in a place they called Pleasant Valley," he says. "There were two families out there that had been feuding for years and trying to get rid of each other, kind of like mafia families, and it was something everybody knew about.

"One day the sheriff came by and said, 'I need your help, somebody got killed on this mine up here.' So I went with him and some others, and we pulled this body out of a pond. The water was all bloody, and the guy had been beaten up really bad, and someone had obviously thrown him in there.

"It turned out that the guy we pulled out had been the last living member of one of those feuding families. A little while later I read where they just ruled that he had drowned."

A few years later, back in Odessa, Townsend and three coworkers decided to use their vacation time on a trip to Alaska.

"They were all talking like, 'Hey, we just may never come back,'" Townsend says, "and I was just going along to see what it was like. They all went back to Odessa within three weeks, and I stayed up there 25 years.

"I got a job with an oil company, and one of the first things I did was call back to Odessa and talk Ramona into coming up there so we could get married. I had met her when she was working as a cashier at a club there, and we had been dating for a while.

"Best decision I ever made."

Alaska was a good life, he says, but he finally retired from the oil business, and he and Ramona came back for a retirement in Texas and now live in Kerrville. Tracey is married to a chief in the Navy and currently lives in Virginia and Mickey is still in Alaska, "doing a lot of fishing."

In July 2002, while playing golf with friends, Townsend began to have chest pains, and when he got home, Ramona decided he needed to go to the hospital in San Antonio.

"I kind of blacked out, and when I came to, I could hear a helicopter," he recalls. "At first I didn't realize I was riding in it.

"After examining me, the doctor decided we could get by with a stint instead of doing a bypass, and they put a pacemaker in. But it just went crazy and I started having spasms with it, so they took it out and put in another, and it didn't work, either.

"The doctor said it was because my heart was so big they couldn't get anything else in there. So I guess you could say I'm a guy with a big heart, ha, ha.

"They finally put two of the three apparatuses in and left one out. I feel okay, but I haven't been back out on the golf course."

Then there was a bad business deal involving two restaurants, in Austin and San Antonio.

"We got into this deal with this Arab guy, and we invested a lot of money in it, and then he went bankrupt," Townsend says. "I've always basically trusted people, and sometimes it doesn't work out very well. We were pretty comfortable before it happened, but this has been a big blow."

More recently came the diagnosis from another doctor that Townsend is in the early stages of Alzheimer's.

"He gave me some tests, and I guess I didn't do too well," Townsend says. "He's talking about memory loss being the start. My wife says I've been absent-minded ever since she's known me, and she doesn't believe this is Alzheimer's.

"As far as how I feel right now goes, I feel fine. Maybe I just don't have much of a future."

Where Have You Gone?

JOHNNY TREADWELL

On the sultry evening of October 20, 1962, the air hung over Memorial Stadium like a blanket of doom—and for most of the 64,000 patrons, the night seemed to grow a little darker with each passing moment.

Here were the seventh-ranked Arkansas Razorbacks—commonly referred to as "seething Hogs" in news accounts of the day—sitting on a three-point lead and camped with a first-and-goal at the Texas three-yard line late in the game, on the verge of striking the decisive blow in a desperate battle of unbeatens.

Then, as gloom settled over the stadium and the top-ranked Longhorns called a timeout to regroup, an eloquent voice emerged in the defensive huddle.

"Now," it said, "we've got 'em where we want 'em."

And with those words, Johnny Treadwell became a Longhorn immortal.

"I was standing there when he said that, and it kind of startled me," David McWilliams says, laughing. "I think he was a lot more confident than I was at that point. But he seemed so sure of it; it was like he was in charge."

An intensely physical player, Treadwell was known to his teammates as "Stoneface," because on the field he normally regarded conversation as wasted energy. But when he did speak, people listened.

The full text of his address was, "Down here they can't throw and they can't run wide; they have to come straight at us."

Arkansas soon obliged, sending six-foot-four, 218-pound all-SWC fullback Danny Brabham hurtling through a gap in the line. He was met head-on by Treadwell and fellow linebacker Pat Culpepper—the two Longhorns who best fit the description, "unhinged." They would have tackled a tank if it had rolled through the line.

The famous end zone photo of the event shows the two linebackers slamming into Brabham and standing him straight up as the ball pops free into the end zone, where defensive back Joe Dixon recovered it for a touchback.

"Culpepper stuck his helmet in there and knocked the ball loose," Treadwell says. "I just jumped in to get my picture taken."

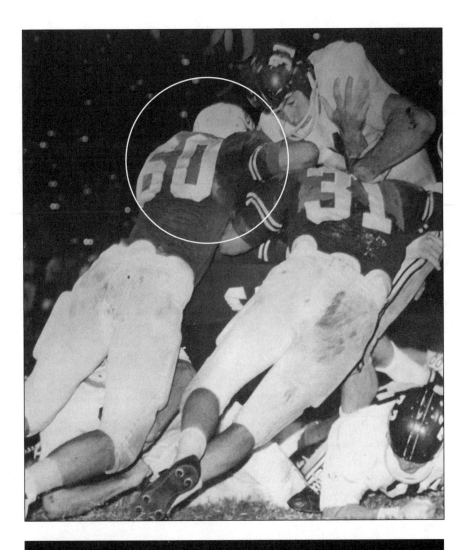

JOHNNY TREADWELL
Hgt: 6-1 • Wgt: 200 • Hometown: Austin

Years played: 1960-1962
Positions: Offensive guard, linebacker
Highlights: 1962: All-SWC, Consensus All-American,
Defensive MVP Cotton Bowl

Johnny Treadwell (*Photo courtesy of the Treadwell family*)

The keen observer, Treadwell says, will find something instructive in the photo.

"If you'll notice, the only three players you can identify are me, Culpepper, and Brabham," he says. "Everyone else is lying flat on the ground. That was by design.

"I was calling the defense, and I called a play—that [defensive coordinator] Mike Campbell and I had talked about—where our linemen went very low at the snap of the ball. Basically, we blocked out the offensive line, and that left no one to protect the ball carrier.

"Danny Brabham ran into that hole naked as a jaybird. Probably still remembers it."

Reprieved, the Longhorns eventually drove 90 yards and scored with 36 seconds left to win 7-3.

In the four decades since, Treadwell's "Now we've got 'em" speech has stood as the emblem of the Darrell Royal teams of the early 1960s. A dynasty built on defense and a casual disdain for adversity—a mindset where defeat seldom intruded.

It has also followed Treadwell—who began the tradition of UT All-Americans wearing the No. 60—throughout his life.

"It's amazing how often it has come up over the years," says Treadwell's wife, Peg. "People always want to talk about it. For instance, I couldn't count how many times someone has told us their church pastor used that story in a sermon to illustrate what determination can achieve when all seems lost."

Treadwell also achieved near-legendary status with his savage play on the field, of which he says, "Well, I found out real early that I wasn't the biggest, the strongest, or the fastest. So I just felt that I needed to play with a little more intensity."

A football star and honor student at nearby Austin High, Treadwell arrived at Texas as a pre-med major. He also believed his football future was as an end.

He was disabused of the latter notion when Campbell—his future guru—said one day, "Treadwell, every time you go out for a pass, you scare me to death."

The desire to become a doctor dissolved in a more wrenching experience: the death of his grandfather—a man who throughout his life carried the affectionate nickname of "Good Time Louie" Peters.

"He died of cancer," Treadwell says. "He was in horrible pain. He wanted to die, but they wouldn't let him. He wasn't the last in my family to suffer that way, and it was something I could never get over.

"The thing that has always stuck with me is when someone holds your hand and says, 'Please, let me go,' they should have the right to make that decision. To die, maybe, with some dignity, if that's possible.

"But that isn't the way it works, and after that experience I knew I could never be a medical doctor."

So he changed his major to veterinary medicine, which meant getting a second degree (after UT) at Texas A&M and beginning a lifelong association with Aggies.

"They're all over this profession, and they've given me hell all these years," Treadwell says, smiling. "Every time I show up at a convention or meeting, it's 'Hey, Tea Sip.'"

It got especially strange once while Treadwell was a student at A&M and the veterinary clinic received a new patient: Bevo, the Texas mascot.

"I forget what his problem was, probably a hoof," Treadwell says, "but they were very secretive about it and basically just snuck him onto campus and then snuck him out again.

"If it had become known around campus that Bevo was there, some of those guys probably would have branded him. Or skinned him."

Before leaving UT, Treadwell began dating Margaret (Peggy) Duke, whose father, renowned chemist Fred Duke, had recently become a professor at A&M.

"We came down from Iowa—I had previously gone to Oberlin and the University of Iowa before my father took the position at A&M," she says. "This was before A&M went coed. There were no women on campus, but I was allowed to take a genetics class because my father was a professor there.

"Having a lone female in the class was kind of hard on the professor—who was a retired colonel, I think—because he had this whole repertoire of dirty jokes he liked to tell to illustrate certain points, and now he couldn't use them. Sometimes he would even say, 'I've got a great joke about this, but I can't tell you.'

"I actually liked him, but I think it was frustrating for him. After the semester, I transferred to Texas."

She later transferred back and completed a master's degree in animal genetics while Treadwell got his degree in veterinary medicine. They were married in 1966 and began establishing a business and raising a family.

"We started out in the cow business," Treadwell says, "with a large outfit servicing the ranching industry. It paid well, but it also meant working 100-hour weeks. Basically, I didn't know my first two kids—they were asleep when I went to work in the morning and asleep when I came back at night.

"Finally, Peg and I sat down and said, 'We've got to do something different.'"

So in 1977 they bought a 100-year-old house with 12-foot ceilings on the corner of 13th and Rio Grande—across the street from old Austin High (which has since moved to a new building)—and began treating domestic pets.

The clinic has done well over the years and so have the Treadwell kids, now numbering four daughters: Leah, 35, went to UT as a merit scholar and is now a medical doctor in Montana; Larah, 34, went to Northern Arizona on a track scholarship and is now the mother of three boys in Tucson; Lochen, 30, went to UT as a merit scholar and now works with the Lower Colorado River Authority in Austin; and Lindsay, 27, went to Notre Dame on a volleyball scholarship, married Mike Rosenthal, now playing tackle for the Minnesota Vikings, and is in her final year of law school.

When time permits, Treadwell usually heads for the woods or the lakes to renew his lifelong love of hunting and fishing.

The Treadwells also keep in touch with old friends, including Darrell Royal. Actually, it was Edith Royal who came by one day with the two orange-and-white cats, a couple of feisty dudes named Waylon and Willie.

But after treating the cats, the Treadwells had to gently drop a little news on Edith: an extensive examination had firmly established that both Waylon and Willie were young ladies.

Where Have You Gone?

JULIUS WHITTIER

In the city of Dallas, if you are young, have problems with the authorities, and feel that a skilled defense attorney is your major priority, Julius Whittier is a good man to call.

Be advised, however, that you may wind up with more than you bargained for.

Whittier, who began his legal career 25 years ago as a prosecutor with the district attorney's office, will provide you with top-grade legal representation at reasonable rates. He will also urge you to confront some hard questions about your life—and what you can do to change it.

"A lot of people think a criminal case is the problem," he says, "and it is, if it's a death penalty case.

"But other than that, most cases represent a symptom of a lifestyle. Even if you're not guilty, it represents some kind of symptom of the way you live. I try to engage my clients in a discussion of why they're here.

"From their standpoint, the opening premise usually is, 'I didn't do anything.' Which logically leads to the question, 'Then why does the DA's office think you did?'

"A discussion of the case then leads us to the 'What is our next step?' phase, at which point I may say, 'We probably need to figure out why you think it makes sense to waste your life, and what you're going to do to change that.'"

If this makes Whittier sound a bit unusual for a defense lawyer, it is understandable. Most of his life has been a little unusual.

In 1970 he became the first black football player ever to earn a letter at the University of Texas and wound up playing on three Cotton Bowl teams. He earned a degree in philosophy and a graduate degree in public affairs, wound up in Boston doing labor relations work for the city for two years, and then came back to UT and entered law school.

In 1981 he went to work for Henry Wade as a prosecutor in the Dallas DA's office and stayed eight years. He has been in private practice—on the defense side

JULIUS WHITTIER
Hgt: 6-0 • Wgt: 295 • Hometown: San Antonio

Years played: 1970-1972
Position: Tight end
Highlights: 1970: Became the first black player to earn a football letter at
Texas; played several positions on three Cotton Bowl teams; starting tight
end as a senior on a team that finished with a No. 3 national ranking

with some civil cases—for the past 15 years, and once conducted an unsuccessful campaign for a judgeship.

He took the scholarship to Texas for the educational opportunity and the chance to play football, not to blaze a trail or become an agent of social change.

But as the child of Oncy and Loraine Whittier growing up in a diverse and rapidly changing environment in San Antonio, he was certainly aware of it.

"I was aware of things that were going on at the time, because they had affected members of my family," he says. "But I had grown up in what was largely an integrated culture. Actually, I had a great childhood.

"My folks provided a great home for us, but they were different in their approach to race relations and the impending clash of cultures ….

"My dad was a doctor—general practitioner. He was a quiet kind of guy: His idea was do your thing, speak with your skill, and let society change itself.

"My Mom was a schoolteacher, politician, and activist. She had us all register with the NAACP when we were kids.

"They were also different in another way: My dad was a sharecropper's son, black as East Texas dirt. My mom was half-Cherokee and half-German, and very light-skinned.

"And she was a firebrand. Once when her father was visiting us—he had light skin, like her—he took some of us kids into a Dairy Queen for some ice cream and Cokes while mom waited in the car.

"The waitress comes out and sees him sitting there with three black kids and told him he could be served inside, but we would have to go to the outside window.

"So when we came back to the car with no ice cream, my mom figured out what happened. She went inside and chewed out everyone working there and then wrote letters to the corporate office.

"It was incredible, the number of things my mom got involved in. She was the first woman to run for a place on the school board [she lost]. She was on the board of the local orphanage. She was a Red Cross volunteer. She started a black teachers' credit union.

"In later years she was one of a group of women, of mixed race, who started a credit union just for women. It was a time when more and more women were becoming heads of households and they couldn't get credit. So some of them got together and basically said, 'Instead of sitting around crying and moaning about it, we'll just start our own credit union.' And they did.

"There was an occasion when HUD put out some grant money to study the problems of women in the mortgage lending industry, and my mom was the person they contacted to put together seminars and discussion groups. She went around to get input from black ministers, the NAACP, Hispanic groups, and others to provide perspectives and coherent ideas about where to look for problems and how to solve them."

But while he was growing up, Whittier says, his main focus was on having fun.

"San Antonio was a great place to grow up," he says. "Probably more progressive than most places around the state at that time, maybe a little unique.

"There wasn't much overt segregation. We could go to the zoo, the library, the stores downtown, go down and swim in San Pedro Park. There was a lot to do, and we did it all.

"There was also free-market bussing. Every kid in the city could go to whatever school they wanted to. You could get transfer cards and bus yourself across town if you wanted. I did that every day. It also meant that there was a kind of natural integration. I went to a high school, Highlands, that was about 80 percent white."

But as Whittier neared the end of his high school days, some of the realities of the "impending culture clash" began to manifest themselves.

"My two sisters got the first taste of it when they went to work at a Handy Andy store," he said. "The cashiers' jobs, which paid more, were not open to black girls.

"So my mom organized a protest, we picketed the store, and my sisters were finally promoted to being cashiers.

"Also about that time, my oldest sister was going with a guy who went to Trinity [University] on a football scholarship, and some incidents began occurring. The mainstream papers weren't keen on reporting racial incidents then, but the local black press did. Eventually the guy nearly got killed. Someone tried to run over him with a car."

Finally, one hit home a little harder.

"My older brother, Oncy," he says, "had joined the Black Guerrilla Theatre group, which would stage political commentary type dramas and skits at the old Ritz Theater, which also housed a local office of the Student Non-Violent Coordinating Committee. Some of their skits would mimic the way the police were perceived in the black community.

"One night the police raided the place, and a lot of people were beaten and arrested. Oncy was beaten in the head by the police, and we had to go get him out of jail.

"It was generally felt that maybe the police were looking for the people from SNCC or maybe just out to crack some heads and see to it that blacks 'stayed in their place.'

"So I was more aware of things by the time I was ready to go to college. Including the fact that I was not the best athlete or the best student. Oncy was, and he was more worldly than me, more forward thinking.

"I was just the one who happened to graduate at the right moment."

And at that time, Whittier says, "I was a 'today' type of guy—pretty much blessed not to worry about tomorrow.

"Did I have a goal in mind? The times I had been to Austin before, it was tagging along with Oncy and his friends, chasing girls over on the East Side. To me, Austin was just a fun place.

"There was a black player there—a freshman named Leon O'Neal—who showed me around, and I just felt so at home. By the time I got there in the fall, Leon had transferred, but I think it was an academic thing.

"I wasn't worried about going to school with white kids, I'd already done that. I wasn't worried about the football part of it, and at that time I really hadn't thought much about the academic part. I wasn't worried about anything.

"I just figured I was going to have a lot of fun. My goal was to have a good time."

Whittier stayed four years, played several positions, and finished as a starting tight end on a team that won the Cotton Bowl. In his final game, he caught a 16-yard pass on the winning touchdown drive.

Julius Whittier (*Photo courtesy of Julius Whittier*)

"Was I aware that I was doing something that hadn't been done there?" he says. "Every day.

"But it was never really much of an issue. I relied on what Darrell Royal and Mike Campbell told me—if you grade out, you play. And they were true to their word. If I had a problem, I could go talk to Coach Royal about it.

"I was interviewed a lot, and I always tried to be honest with the reporters. But really, I wasn't having a problem."

At Texas, Whittier found awareness of a different sort.

"UT was like a second birth for me—an awakening," he says. "My eyes were opened to a wider world, which amazed me and fascinated me. There was so much to do, so many courses of study, so much knowledge. It overwhelmed me. I loved it.

"In fact, I loved UT so much that I went to school there—for at least part of the year—each year between 1969 and 1980. I got two degrees and an invaluable appreciation of the world around me.

"As far as being in a racially-charged environment is concerned, I had to go all the way to Boston to encounter a situation where someone called me a nigger and I didn't respond.

"You know, growing up in the neighborhood, if some guy had a beef with you, he might use that word just to get you to fight. So we'd get it on and get it over with, and that was the end of it.

"But in Boston it went a lot deeper than that. There are ideas—and people—up there that are just crazy. Culturally, it's the other end of the earth."

Whittier also had a few problems with the job.

"I was hired to do labor relations for the city, and they sent me to Boston City Hospital, where they had a serious problem with chronic absenteeism. There were people who had 270 days absent in a year and still had a job.

"I was sent to process them through the termination procedure, and I processed a lot of people. But when I left two years later, only eight people had left the payroll."

Whittier laughs.

"Those Irish boys really had that one tied up," he says.

So Whittier came back to Texas and began preparing for a career in law. Having spent considerable time with both prosecution and defense, he says he has enjoyed both.

"Oh, definitely, the appeal of being a prosecutor is that you're wearing a white hat," he says. "You embody the righteous indignation of the people in the battle against crime. You are an avenging deity, crying for justice for the widows and families of the dead.

"One of the things about violent crimes is that usually, sorting out the motive is fairly easy—greed, passion, relationships with other people, appetites out of control, depression, or low self-esteem, people wanting more than they make: all the things the Greeks wrote about 3,000 years ago.

"On the defense side, it's very gratifying to have a client who is innocent and be able to get that client off. In the other case, I try to get my clients to talk about what is seriously wrong in their lives.

"Sometimes the reasons for our actions are not the sort of noble things you can put on a banner: 'I stole because I'm greedy, because I don't want a regular job, because I'm too good to work for $6 an hour. I had to—I had no other way to eat.'

"Okay, let's talk about that. Why don't you have any other way to eat? How can we change that? That's kind of the approach I use."

Does it work?

"Well, one of my former clients is about to enter law school," Whittier says, smiling. "Of course, he's one of the ones who was innocent."

Whittier is divorced and has two daughters, Cheyenne, 10, and Olivia Katherine, four.

BOBBY WUENSCH

When Bobby Wuensch suffered a serious neck injury in the spring of his freshman year at the University of Texas, he dutifully followed all of the procedures that usually accompany such a problem.

He went to be examined by several doctors, a couple of whom told him he should never play football again. He allowed them to put him in traction. He followed all of the usual advice until it seemed that nothing was getting better.

Then, he did something rather unusual for a teenage athlete: He cured the injury himself.

"It had been a while, and it seemed like nothing had changed much, so I figured out a way to rehabilitate it myself," he says. "In the process I taught myself something: that you can rehabilitate your health in a lot of different ways if you just think about it and work at it.

"So I started doing some different type stuff with my neck. Me and my dad took a football helmet and screwed it into a 35-pound lead weight, and I would put it on and exercise with it.

"I would lay on my back and raise my head, then turn over and do the same thing lying on my stomach, and I would roll over on each side and do it. Pretty soon, the neck started getting stronger, and the pain went away, and eventually I was back to normal."

But Wuensch, who is now back in Houston running the family business—Wuensch Sales—with his sister, Maureen, recalls that the conventional treatment prescribed by the doctors had its positive side.

"Sometimes when I would be getting treatment at the university medical center," he says, "Greg Lott would be in there rehabbing a knee, and his girlfriend, Farrah Fawcett, would come visit him. I never said a word to her, but I enjoyed it."

But although Wuensch may never have conversed with Farrah, he did come out of the deal with a new companion.

BOBBY WUENSCH

Hgt: 6-3 • Wgt: 220 • Hometown: Houston

Years played: 1968-1970
Position: Offensive tackle
Highlights: 1969: All-SWC, All-American;
1970: All-SWC, Consensus All-American

"I took that helmet with me wherever I went throughout my career," he says. "I took it with me on the road—even when we went to California—and I worked out with it every day to keep my neck strong."

There was, however, one life-altering aspect of the injury.

A two-way player coming out of Houston Jones as an All-State selection (and teammate of future UT All-American Bill Atessis) after the 1965 season, Wuensch considered himself basically a middle linebacker and strongly identified Tommy Nobis as his ultimate role model.

"He was so great," Wuensch says, "and he was one of the most visible players in the country at that point—they had won a national championship in 1963. So, yeah, I kind of wanted to go to UT and see what kind of middle linebacker I could be—that's where I played in all the All-Star games—largely because of Tommy Nobis.

"But when I came back after rehabbing the neck injury, I was a little timid about sticking my neck in there as a linebacker. So they moved me to the offensive line."

Although it is interesting to speculate on what kind of middle linebacker Wuensch might have been, the kind of offensive lineman he became is a matter of record: a two-time All-American and a consensus pick his senior year.

But then, Wuensch was always destined for stardom. This was a man, after all, who had once played in the Strawberry Bowl.

"One of my greatest thrills," he says, laughing. "It was when I was in the seventh grade, playing on a Little League football team coached by Teddy Scruggs, an old Rice star. We won a championship, and they sent us to Pasadena, California, to play in a bowl game, and that's what they called it. We were all thrilled."

He may also have been predestined to wind up at UT, even without the Nobis angle.

"The coach at Jones was W.C. Treadway, another old Rice star, the kind of guy you'd run through a wall for," Wuensch says. "We were called the Golden Falcons, but somehow we wound up wearing orange jerseys and running the Texas Power Sweep a lot.

"Then when Darrell Royal actually came around to recruit me, I was stunned. I thought, 'Gee, if he really thinks I'm good enough to play at Texas, that's it. I'm going.'

"Of course, with unlimited scholarships, what they did back then was just go out and get the 50 best guys they could sign—but I didn't know that.

"Going to Texas gave me the opportunity to compete against the best, and that's always meant a lot to me. The unfortunate thing was that we had a lot of good athletes who never got to play. They went on to get their education, but they might have excelled somewhere else.

"But Coach Royal was really impressive, and still is. A few years ago one of my nieces was up there at a game and she saw him sitting in a limo, and she went running up to the window and told him she was my niece, and he talked to her for a few minutes.

"Then when she was leaving he rolled the window back down and said, 'Hey, tell Butch and Opal hello.' Amazing—after 30 years he still remembered my parents' names."

Although Wuench's offensive position in high school had been center, he figured 1968 was a good year to switch to tackle at Texas because of a revolutionary new offense called the Wishbone, which he still refers to as the Veer. Whatever it was, it knocked the college football world on its kiester.

"It was incredible," he says. "Starting the season we tied Houston and lost to Texas Tech, and then won nine straight. I still think that was the best team we had, but we kept winning for two more years. Because of the injury, I had taken a red-shirt year, so I played in every one of those 30 straight wins we had. It was like being in a dream."

Ironically, Wuench quickly lost his fear of using his head in combat.

"For guys like me and Bob McKay, the great thing about that offense was that it made us truly 'offensive' linemen. If I had spent my career trying to drop back a step and pass-block, I would have never been successful.

"But we didn't have to do that much. Mostly, it was just hitting the defensive guy head on and driving him back. Just stick your helmet in his face and get it done."

Then the *real* fun began.

"After I blocked my guy," he says, "I would go down the line, and if I caught some guy sleeping, I'd hit him, and McKay was doing the same thing. Or if a guy was going for a tackle, I'd try to hit him and spring the back, or go downfield and block. But it didn't matter if they were making a tackle or not, we knocked 'em down anyway.

"We became famous for that. You have to play the whole game."

As the games rolled by in those years, the Longhorns weren't merely victorious, they were scary. Weird, even. But it went much deeper than cocky.

"This year, when we had the reunion of the teams from that famous 1969 game up in Arkansas," he says, "one of the Arkansas players started talking about something that amazed them in that game.

"He talked about how they would watch us when we came to the line of scrimmage in the second half, when we were down 14 points and being frustrated offensively and seemingly on our way to defeat in the big game. They were a little stunned that there was no dissension, no name-calling, no grumbling, no frazzled looks. He said we never seemed rattled—always calm, cool, collected.

"And that's the way we were. After 1968, I never went onto the field for a game with the thought that we might lose.

"But of course, the big story of that Arkansas game was our defense, which played the way Texas always plays defense. It had been the bread and butter of the program for years, but it had been kind of overlooked because we scored so much."

Not to be overlooked, however, is Wuensch's memorable contribution to the postgame scene in the locker room. There it is, filmed and on tape: Wuensch patting Richard Nixon on the shoulder.

"I really don't know why I did that," he says, laughing. "I just wanted to meet him, and I was excited and elated, because all of a sudden we really were the champs. I just did it out of elation."

By this time it had become accepted among teammates that Wuensch—normally a polite, well-mannered individual prone to addressing people as "Sir"—became a different human being in the heat of battle. The usual result was something a bit more forceful than a pat on the shoulder.

The ultimate manifestation of this phenomenon occurred less than a month later in the Cotton Bowl game against Notre Dame. Like many teammates, Wuensch professes to have been shocked and offended by what they regarded as unsportsmanlike conduct on the part of the Fighting Irish, which included trash talk and attempts as physical intimidation.

Wuensch's response to this came early in the game, after Mike Dean, Texas' 195-pound right guard, threw a block that flattened the biggest man on the field, massive Notre Dame tackle Mike McCoy.

So, Bobby, how is it that a sensitive lad like yourself wound up walking over to McCoy, yanking him up by his facemask, announcing, "Mike Dean is gonna kick your butt all day!" and then slamming him back down to the ground?

"Well—ah—that was a different kind of trash talking," Wuensch says, laughing. "Actually, I consider it a form of leadership—demonstrating my confidence to my 200-pound teammate that he can whip that 300-pound guy all day, which he did.

"Okay, I guess that, in those situations I kind of underwent a personality change."

The Longhorns won that game 21-17, but a year later it was a different story. In Wuensch's final game, Notre Dame finally broke Texas' 30-game winning streak with a 24-11 win.

"It wasn't the end of the world," he says. "We won 30 straight, and I was there for all of it. How could you ask for a greater thrill than that?"

Wuensch was drafted in the 12th round by Baltimore, which had already drafted his buddy Atessis in the second round. That was another thrill for Wuensch, but his NFL career lasted for four exhibition games and ended with a broken leg.

"In the fourth game, I was going down on a punt return," he says, "and got leg-whipped by one of my own teammates. He caught me with my leg planted, and it broke the shinbone in half.

"It swelled up pretty bad, and I was in the hospital for a few days, then I went home for three weeks. Eventually I rejoined the team, but I couldn't play, of course. They paid me off after the wildcard game, and I went home. The next June I was working out, and it suddenly dawned on me that I didn't want to do this anymore.

"To tell you the truth, I think I was relieved. Pro ball was different, and I had gained 25 pounds and didn't really feel that mobile anymore. Plus, I wasn't real skilled at pass blocking.

"It was a thrill just to be drafted, to have that experience, to meet all those players I'd read about for years. Heck, they don't even have a 12th round anymore."

So he stayed in Houston and went to work for Wuensch Sales, the family business his parents—Raymond (Butch) and Opal Wuensch—began in the shipyards in 1963.

The company's business is selling marine supplies. The clientele consists of the huge ocean-going ships that arrive in the port of Houston every hour of every day.

"In the beginning we used to chase the ships—foreign vessels, usually—that came into the port," he says. "Then about 10 or 15 years ago we went wholesale, and life got a little easier. Chasing ships was a 24-7 job, and it was wild.

"What I mean by that is, the Ship Channel is 52 miles long and we literally chased the ships [with trucks] when they came in, with supplies we had contracted for. If a ship docks at midnight, that's when you load it. We served a lot of the big chemical tankers then, and we were literally running around like crazy a lot of the time, but I liked it. I was a whole lot younger then.

"In time, we procured a lot of buying power and went wholesale. We have a warehouse on Navigation Boulevard, a stone's throw from the Turning Basin, and we have a very diversified customer base now.

"We service the stevedores, we service the terminals, we service the ship channelers—we do some retail and a lot of wholesale, and we get a lot of off-shore business. We're turning 41 this year, and people know who we are. We're very service oriented."

In time the younger generation took over from the elders. Wuensch now runs the business with his sister, Maureen.

"I'm the general manager, and she's the comptroller," he says. "I handle operations, and she handles the money.

"It's been an interesting life. It's allowed me to learn to deal with people, and it's been an education. I've gotten to be pretty good at communicating with people who don't speak English. I've made friends of all kinds—Norwegians, Swedes, Danes, a lot of Scandinavians, and Asian folks."

Somewhere back there, he also found time to marry Donna, his best friend's wife.

"Actually, I've known her since she was 14," he says, "and I was the best man at her first marriage—which was to a good buddy of mine. So, I don't know what that says for my character.

"Seriously, I didn't break up her marriage—we didn't start dating until after the divorce. We've been married 30 years and have a son, David, who is 27 and a 2000 UT grad and works for Continental Airlines."

At 57, he says, life is pretty good.

"Back when I was single, I used to go to New Orleans some," he says, "and I've kind of started up again. Maureen and her husband have been riding in the Mardi Gras Parade for 20 years, and about six years ago we started going with them.

"It's fun if you like to watch people and party a little bit. Donna and Maureen like to go to Harrah's and gamble.

"Business is steady, so we're doing well. Maureen has three kids and three grandchildren, so there's a big extended family. My dad died in 2001. My mom is 77 and facing a toe amputation—she's a diabetic. I'm diabetic, too, but I'm not insulin-dependent. I weigh about 260 now, but I try to exercise and watch my diet.

"The experience we all had at Texas years ago … sometimes people will hear your name and come up and start talking to you. I guess it's kind of like a little badge of honor we all carry with us. The thing I enjoyed most was the camaraderie between us. It was a special time.

"I was just glad to be there."